Blue-Collar Leadership® & Supervision

Mack Story

DEDICATION

To those with the courage to accept a leadership position, especially those who did it without any leadership training.

When you look at your leader, what do you see?

When your team looks at you, what do they see?

What you know matters.

Who you are matters more.

CONTENTS

ACKNOWLEDGMENTS

I would like to thank the many front line, blue-collar leaders who helped me accomplish some amazing things in my 20 years in the manufacturing industry, especially those who were team members on the hundreds of kaizen events I led.

Two of the greatest lessons I learned from front line supervisors:

1. The most respected leaders always respect others.

2. The most effective leaders walk through the door to serve their team, not to be served by their team.

1

IN THE BEGINNING...

THE CHALLENGE OF NOT KNOWING
WHAT YOU DON'T KNOW

"Principle-centered people are constantly educated by their experiences. They read, they seek training, they take classes, they listen to others, they learn through both their ears and eyes...they discover that the more they know, the more they realize they don't know." ~ Stephen R. Covey

The more I learn the more I become aware of all that I don't know. More awareness leads to more reading, learning, and applying, which leads to an even higher level of awareness of all that I don't know. It never ends.

I call it *"dumber by the book."* Sure, I learn more with every book, but I also become aware of so much more that I don't know. As I read to increase my knowledge and understanding, I also feel less knowledgeable or *"dumber"* overall because I'm now aware of so much more I don't know but need to know. It happens with every leadership book I read.

In his book, *The 8th Habit*, Stephen R. Covey illustrates our *"circle of knowledge,"* what we do know, as a solid area in the shape of a circle. He also refers to the *"circle of ignorance,"* what we don't know, as everything that's along the outside edge of our *"circle of knowledge."* If we knew those things, they would be in our *"circle of knowledge."* But, we don't know about them. We're only *aware* of them. So, they remain in our *"circle of ignorance."*

I like to call the edge of the *"circle of knowledge"* the *perimeter of awareness*. Along your perimeter of awareness, you find those things you're aware of but don't yet truly know and understand.

There are also many other things you need to know that are currently well beyond your perimeter of awareness. They are in your *area of ignorance.* At the moment, you're completely unaware of them and won't become aware of them until you expand your *"circle of knowledge."* There's a good chance you're expanding it right now.

When your *"circle of knowledge"* expands, your perimeter of awareness automatically expands. As it does, you become aware of some things previously in your area of ignorance. Those are the things you didn't know you didn't know. You still don't know them. But at least now, you know that you need to know. In other words, your awareness has increased.

If you choose to learn about those things, you grow and the cycle repeats. If you choose not to learn about them, you're done growing. When you're done growing, you're done. At best, you stay where you are. At worst, you begin to slip backward and get passed over by those that choose continuous growth.

The more we know, the more we realize what we don't know. Interestingly, learning this principle provides us with a new perspective of what's going on within us and others.

Those among us that think they know it all, don't know much *at all.* They have a *tiny "circle of knowledge"* (about the size of the period at the end of this sentence) which explains their *tiny* perimeter of awareness. Because *know it alls* don't know much about anything, they're not aware of how much there is to know about everything. Therefore, they think they know it all. They're not necessarily dumb people. They simply have an extremely large area of ignorance.

You can consider your *"circle of knowledge"* generally. Or, you can consider it very specifically. As you read this book, you're increasing your *"circle of knowledge"* very specifically relative to learning leadership principles. Leadership can be defined simply with one word: INFLUENCE.

After 20 years in the manufacturing industry, I resigned from the corporate world in 2008 to launch my own Lean

Manufacturing Consulting firm. At the time, I had worked my way up to the position of Lean Manufacturing and Quality Manager reporting directly to the Plant Manager.

My first 10 years were spent as a front line, entry-level factory worker (CNC machine operator) doing the hard work and responsible only for myself. Then finally, I began to work my way up after starting and eventually graduating from college. Much of that story can be found in my book, *Defining Influence: Increasing Your Influence Increases Your Options.*

I worked my way up from the bottom to second from the top with only one formal leader above me on site. What's interesting is I never received any leadership training. NONE! However, I was asked to and expected to lead others. This happens ALL the time. It may have happened to you.

At the time of my resignation, I was responsible for leading hundreds of people. Few people reported directly to me, but I was responsible for getting all of them to buy-in to process improvements, endless change, and to improve quality.

I wasn't exposed to leadership training until I resigned. I had done well. In my 20 year corporate career, I had been promoted 14 times. I thought I knew a lot about leadership, and I did. But, I still didn't know what I didn't know.

Formal leadership development was in my *area of ignorance.* A friend gave me a one hour leadership audio lesson. He placed it on my *perimeter of awareness.* I listened to it and expanded my *"circle of knowledge"* which also expanded my *perimeter of awareness*, and I began to know what I didn't know.

Odds are high that this may be your first exposure to formal leadership development. Either way, I plan to place a few things on *your* perimeter of awareness. *I hope you're ready.*

"If you have already been trying hard, maybe trying harder is not the way. Try different." ~ Henry Cloud

2

DEMYSTIFYING LEADERSHIP

MOVING BEYOND
MANAGEMENT AND SUPERVISION

"Leadership is about taking responsibility for lives not numbers. Managers look after our numbers and our results, and leaders look after us." ~ Simon Sinek

Wow! Simon nailed it. Unfortunately, the reality is most people experience management instead of leadership.

Is that your reality? How does your boss treat you? Like a person or an object? Does it matter? How does it make you feel? Does it impact your performance? Pause and think about it.

What is *your* team's reality? How do you treat them? Like a person or an object? Would some say a person? Would some say an object? Does it matter?

I'm asking you to look in the mirror. Every high impact leader's journey begins *in the mirror*. Most likely, you found it easier to look out the window at your boss than to look in the mirror at yourself. Choosing to be a high impact leader isn't easy. You must do a lot of work on the inside if you want to be highly effective on the outside.

I refer to the leaders Simon described above as *high impact* leaders. I hope you are one or choose to become one. Also, any reference to the term manager when discussing the leadership of people is purely related to those people who are in a position of authority that choose to continue treating their team members like objects, instead of like people. Those managers either don't value high impact leadership (I can't help them at all), or they simply don't know what they don't know

(I can help them a lot).

High impact leaders look after their people. Managers always look after themselves and rarely, if ever, look after their people beyond what is required. This book is *not* about the management of people or the supervision of people. Anyone can manage and supervise if they have a position of power and the authority to do so. This book *is* about helping you become highly effective as a high impact leader.

Don't misunderstand me. Unless you are the absolute top leader in the organization, you *must* be a manager of things and processes. And, you *should* be a leader of people. However, if you are the top leader and you want to only lead, you can always hire others to do all of the managing of things and processes for you with a few exceptions along the way.

To say it simply, we *must* manage things and processes because they don't think or feel. But, we *should* lead people because they do think and feel. Unfortunately, when you have a position of authority, you can take the easy road and choose to *manage* the people too. Or, at least, you can until they do some thinking and change departments or work addresses. When that happens, you can no longer manage *or* lead them. We choose our actions, but not our consequences.

During my 20 years in the blue-collar workforce before I started my own consulting business, I didn't work with many high impact leaders. I can actually count them on one hand and still have a few fingers left over. And, I remember them all. All the rest chose to manage those of us that worked *for* them.

You don't work *for* high impact leaders. You work *with* them. They know it, and you know it. You don't work *with* managers. You work *for* them. They know it, and you know it.

Is your boss a manager or a high impact leader? Most likely, you knew the answer instantly because you've already been thinking about it. I hope you've also been thinking about this question too: *"Do those who report to me work for a manager or with a high impact leader?"*

They already know the answer just as you already knew the answer about your boss before you started reading this book.

I've simply provided some new terms and some new ways of looking at it.

How do you know when you're in the presence of a high impact leader? It's simple. You'll feel it. How do you know when you're in the presence of a manager? It's simple. You'll feel it. However, what you feel in each case will be tremendously different. The leader will generally leave you feeling good. The manager will generally leave you feeling not so good.

The question you need to ask yourself at this point is: Do I want to become a more effective leader of people, a high impact leader? If yes, you're in for a treat. Because I'm going to share some golden nuggets of wisdom that will help you launch your career as a high impact leader, *if you apply them.*

Many of these nuggets I learned during my 11,000 hours of leading cross-functional teams through process improvement, organizational change, and cultural transformation, without a position of direct authority over any of the team members. I was an outsider, a consultant, hired to lead groups of strangers. Most of the time they didn't want to change, so I had to build trust and influence them to buy-in to me first and my vision second. We always achieved amazing results together.

Many of these nuggets will also come from the hundreds of leadership books I have read, the thousands of hours of leadership audios I have listened to, and the numerous leadership seminars I have attended. I have validated what I'm sharing with you by first applying it in my professional life at work and also my personal life at home.

I hope becoming a high impact leader excites you, it should. If so, you must be prepared to climb the leadership mountain.

"A true leader has the confidence to stand alone, the courage to make tough decisions, and the compassion to listen to the needs of others. He does not set out to be a leader, but becomes one by the equality of his actions and the integrity of his intent." ~ Douglas MacArthur

3

CLIMBING THE
LEADERSHIP MOUNTAIN

YOU'VE BEEN GIVEN A LEADERSHIP
POSITION, BUT WILL YOU LEAD?

*"Management is about persuading people to do things
they do not want to do, while leadership is about
inspiring people to do things they never
thought they could." ~ Steve Jobs*

Will you move beyond management and supervision and
choose to lead? Will you be become bigger than your position?

Unfortunately, very few front line bosses are expected to
lead. Most often, their boss isn't leading them and doesn't
know much about high impact leadership themselves. Far too
often, their goal is to just make it through the day.

I wrote this book to help you help yourself. I've been
mining leadership nuggets for years, so my intent on these
pages is to remove the dirt and give you page after page of
pure gold relative to accelerating your leadership climb.
Although this is a short and simple book, it is a tremendously
powerful tool of transformation if learned and applied. Soak it
up. Highlight or underline the key points. Use it as a tool, and
reference it as you grow. Don't give it away.

If this is your first leadership book, you will discover that
becoming a high impact leader has *little* to do with your boss
developing you and *everything* to do with *you* developing
yourself. The leadership mountain is always there waiting to be
climbed. However, *you must choose* to climb it.

No company or boss ever invested a single dollar on

leadership development for me. They all expected me to be a good manager, and I was. But, I also chose to become a leader of people without realizing exactly what I was doing at the time. And once I discovered what you'll learn from this book, which took me many years, I began to accelerate my climb up the leadership mountain. It's a privilege for me to help you do the same.

If you're fortunate enough to work with a high impact leader, you have a huge advantage over those who don't because you will have tremendous support during your climb. You will have someone come along-side you to not only *help* you grow and develop as a leader, but they will also continue to grow and develop *with* you.

What does it mean to be given a position? It means someone believes you have potential. That's a good thing. Congratulations! You have been plucked from the forest and placed at the bottom of the leadership mountain. Notice, I didn't say placed at the top of the leadership mountain. Far too often, someone who does a good job is simply offered a position of authority: team leader, line lead, lead man, supervisor, manager, etc. In other words, they become a boss.

Position has a lot to do with managing things, processes, and people, but it has very little to do with leading people.

Managing people from a position of authority is about motivating them to do what is expected. Motivation comes from the outside, from someone else. When you're effective, you're considered a highly effective manager.

But, leading people is about inspiring them to choose to do more than expected, to do it better than expected, and to do it before it's expected. Inspiration comes from within.

What does it take to climb the leadership mountain and to grow beyond your position? First, you must be able to responsibly and effectively manage the things and processes in your area of responsibility. Managing is about what you know and what you can do: ability, skills, knowledge, etc. Managing is something you *must* do. It is a job *requirement*. If you don't do it, your boss will find someone else who will. You will then be removed from the base of the leadership mountain and cast back into the forest. *You must master your position.*

Managers stop there. They think mastering their position is the goal. To become a high impact leader, you must continue to climb. You begin by building solid relationships on a foundation of trust. It's not about position. It's about people. Building relationships has a little to do with what you know, competency, and a lot to do with who you are, character.

As you build trust, people become inspired by you instead of driven by you. Your influence increases far beyond what comes with your position. You still have your position, but now you're leading with influence instead of managing with authority. This increased influence with your team translates into better results: increased engagement, retention, and productivity along with improved morale and teamwork. When you make a bigger difference, your leadership *will* be noticed.

If you've managed to climb this high, you're now at the top of the leadership mountain. You are a great leader, but you're not a high impact leader. High impact leaders do more than successfully climb the leadership mountain. You may be wondering, *"If I'm at the top, what else can I do?"*

What separates high impact leaders from great leaders is this. High impact leaders don't stand on top of the mountain and enjoy the view. High impact leaders go back down the mountain and help others navigate their way to the top, just as I'm doing with you right now. Climbing the leadership mountain is about success, but helping others climb the leadership mountain is about significance.

When you're able to climb to the top of the leadership mountain, then go back down and effectively help others climb their way to the top, you will be a high impact leader.

I'll now begin helping you navigate your way to the top of the leadership mountain. Once we're there, I'll also help you go back down and bring some others up with you. *Let's climb.*

"To excel in leadership, you must first master followership."
~ Truett Cathy

4

UNDERSTANDING ARTIFICIAL INFLUENCE

THERE IS A DIFFERENCE BETWEEN SOMEONE RESPECTING YOUR POSITION AND SOMEONE RESPECTING YOU

"Into the hands of every individual is given a marvelous power for good or evil - the silent, unconscious, unseen influence of his life. This is simply the constant radiation of what man really is, not what he pretends to be."
~ William George Jordan

If you want to begin to lead beyond your position, you must be respected by those you want to influence. No one gives you respect. You can demand respect all day long, but it's a waste of time. I always laugh (on the inside) when I hear someone demand respect. You will never be respected because you demand to be respected, at work or at home. It's simply not going to happen.

Think about it from your own point of view. If there's a boss or manager you don't like because of who they are as a person, can they demand respect from you and get it? Absolutely not. You may respect their position. But, you will never respect them simply because they demand it. You *must* respect their position to *keep* your job. But, you don't have to respect *them* to keep your job.

A position will give you authority but not influence. Influence must be earned by first earning respect. The more you are respected the more influence you will gain. Everything I'm sharing in this book, *if applied*, will help you earn respect and increase your influence with others.

10

Having a position or title such as Mom, Dad, Coach, Boss, Supervisor, Manager, VP, President, CEO, Owner, etc. gives you authority and control over other people. I call this *artificial influence*. Artificial influence creates the *illusion* that you have *authentic* influence. However, if you choose to influence people using only artificial influence, you are not leading. You are simply managing. Sure you may accomplish a lot, but what are you leaving on the table?

You can easily validate the principle of artificial influence by considering those bosses you've had, or now have, that you would never follow if they didn't control your pay, your time off, your promotions, etc. If you only follow a boss because you *have to*, their influence is *not* authentic. It's artificial. And unfortunately for the company, most likely, you will only do what you have to do.

The title of boss is one that is simply given, often by another manager with artificial influence. However, when it comes to authentic influence, managers are not in the same league as leaders. If you develop authentic influence based on character-based principles that you have internalized, then you will *earn* the right to lead. When you do, those reporting to you will do much *more than they have to* simply because they *respect* you.

A high impact leader operates from a position of authentic influence, not artificial influence or authority.

Listen to the voices of those with *artificial* influence:

- How am I supposed to make something happen when those people don't report to me?
- I can't make them do anything. They don't report to me and won't do anything I tell them to do.
- I can't get anything done in that department. They report to someone else, not me. It's useless to try.
- How can I be responsible for their results when they don't report to me?
- If you want me to make it happen, you've got to give me authority over those people.
- My hands are tied. They don't report to me.

Phrases like those are always spoken by a manager, never by a leader. I've heard them spoken many times in my career by managers who don't have a clue about leadership. The only influence they have at work is directly tied to the authority, *artificial influence*, which is associated with the position they hold. Without it, they wouldn't accomplish much of anything.

I remember being in a facility as a consultant once. I needed some help from a few team members in a different department, so I asked the manager I was working with if it would be okay if I went over and asked them for some help. He said, *"You'll have to wait. I'll have to get an interpreter because none of them speak English."* I said, *"Okay, I'll go wait over there."* I thought it was interesting. When I got there, they all spoke English to me. Leadership is influence.

Managers make things happen with people who *have to* help them. Leaders make things happen with people who *want to* help them.

Most managers have never read a leadership book and can't understand a leader doesn't need authority to make something happen. Leaders only need *influence* to make something happen. Leadership is *not* about who *has* to help you. Leadership *is* about who *wants* to help you.

Research studies have repeatedly shown a 40% productivity increase when comparing people who *want to* follow a leader with those who *have to* follow a manager.

A manager thrives on artificial influence and is not interested in developing himself or others in order to capture this massive loss of productivity. That's what leaders do, not managers.

How do you influence? What is your style? Are you a director or a connector? Do you tell or sell? What would change if you had more authentic influence in every situation?

"When we look at people who disobey their leaders, the first question we ought to ask is not, 'What's wrong with those people?' but rather, 'What's wrong with their leader?' It says that responsibility begins at the top."
~ Malcolm Gladwell

5

DEFINING YOUR LEADERSHIP STYLE

DO OTHERS FOLLOW YOU BECAUSE THEY HAVE TO OR BECAUSE THEY WANT TO?

"I suppose leadership at one time meant muscles; but today it means getting along with people." ~ Mahatma Gandhi

You're given a position, and you're told what and who to manage. But, *how* you lead is up to you. The position does not define you. You define the position. Your *values* will determine if people follow you because they have to or because they want to. It's all about your style. How do you operate?

No one but you can, or will, determine your leadership style. When it comes to climbing the leadership mountain, your leadership style can launch you like a rocket, or it can hold you back like an anchor. *Your values will determine your style.* Who you are on the inside is what people will experience on the outside.

Most often, the managers who hired me when I worked as a process improvement consultant typically thought I was extremely gifted and could do amazing things.

Actually, I usually didn't know very much about what they were doing, how they were doing it, or why they were doing it.

I want to share a story to illustrate two very different leadership styles based on two very different values.

The manager in this story had over 30 years of experience in their operations. I didn't have any.

What I do have is a very effective leadership style that allows me to quickly connect with and influence people. This enables me to get their buy-in quickly, to get them to work together quickly, and to unleash the potential within them that their managers don't even know they have. Any high impact leader can do the same thing.

I was leading a process improvement event as an outside consultant. The team's goal was to redesign the layout of a manufacturing work area to improve the work flow in order to make the process more productive.

A lot of changes were needed. It had been the way it was for many years. I was brought in by the top leaders, so everyone had to play along. They didn't have to change. If they didn't want to, they could have blamed me. They would have been right because I was the leader. I simply wouldn't have been invited back because I *was* ultimately responsible.

When I arrived on Monday morning, I was a stranger. I didn't have any formal authority. I was basically a hired leader, but the manager who hired me didn't understand that. If they would have, they wouldn't have hired me. First of all, they wouldn't have needed me. They would have already developed a team of internal leaders. And secondly, they would be out making things happen themselves.

Remember, I was new to the area. It was my first day on the job working with the team. Everything that happened or didn't happen that week was a direct result of my leadership style. I didn't have a clue about what they were producing. But, I knew they did. Without formal authority, my only option was to lead with influence by applying the principles I'm teaching you in this book. However, I had to do it quickly. I was only going to be with the team from start to finish for five days. We would not be planning. We would be doing.

My style involved coming in on Monday and immediately connecting with the team and conducting leadership training with them. I wanted to get to know them. I wanted them to get to know me. And, I wanted to share key leadership principles to get them in the right mindset to achieve amazing results together. I had done this many times before. It wasn't new for me, but it was new for the manager.

The manager, who was also a team member, had never participated in an event like the one I was leading. He didn't know what he didn't know. However, his style was built on a foundation of pride and ego. He wanted those on the team to know he was the boss. The first thing he did when I started connecting with the team was roll his eyes. He was a manager of people. Then, he proceeded to let the team know we were wasting time. He thought we should be out on the shop floor making changes. After all, in his mind, that was the *only* reason we were there.

The manager's style was to come in and *take control* of the team. My style was to come in and *empower* the team. They had been controlled long enough. The manager's style was to give orders and do all the talking. My style was to ask questions and do all the listening. This was the type of environment where I truly learned to be a high impact leader. Situations like this were common as I built up over 11,000 hours of experience leading cross-functional teams like this through change.

Don't miss the point, this manager *"owned"* the area. He could have already made any changes he wanted. He didn't want changes. But, if changes were going to be made, he wanted to be in charge of those making them. Managers value being in control. Leaders value the team being in control.

I immediately focused on building trust with the team. I also ignored the manager's need for control and leveraged his strengths to benefit the team. He was there all week, but he had very little influence beyond his authority. He wanted to be in charge, and formally was, but I had the most influence. Positive influence trumps negative authority every time.

We made it happen in spite of his inability to lead and his desire to manage. He didn't have to know how to lead that week, I was doing the leading. He simply needed to follow.

The team delivered amazing results! They already had all the answers and knew what needed to be done. They simply hadn't been allowed to do it. My style of leadership released them. The manager's style had suppressed them. *Style matters, and it matters a lot!*

> *"Nobody wants a boss. Everyone wants a coach."*
> *~ Art Williams*

6

HIGH IMPACT LEADERSHIP

LEADERSHIP STARTS WITH YOU,
BUT IT'S NOT ABOUT YOU

"What stands between you and your goal is your behavior."
~ Darren Hardy

It's a very good sign for you and your team that you have made it this far into the book. This means you're interested in high impact leadership.

You're also already far ahead of the pack. Most people in a position of authority will never pick up a leadership book, much less read one. They will never know what they don't know. But, you *will* know what they don't know. You are giving yourself an advantage every time you read a page.

As you begin to apply what they don't know, you will quickly begin to separate yourself from the traditional managers. Your influence will begin to increase left and right and up and down. You will become a 360° leader with influence in every direction. You will become much more valuable to your organization and to other organizations that value high impact leaders.

However, to increase your leadership ability you must do much more than show interest and read this book. You must take action. *Leadership starts with you, but it's not about you.* You must act. Then, influence others to act.

My intent so far has been to begin to paint a picture in your mind's eye, a picture of *why* you should grow as a leader. Since you're still with me, I'm hoping it's because you can see the picture clearly now and are anxious to learn more, so you can grow beyond your current position and title. I also hope you are beginning to realize the potential that lies within you to get better as a person which will make you better as a leader.

I'll begin focusing on *how* to grow as a leader and *what* you should do to grow as a leader. I'll continue to provide some of the *why* behind it all too. I can tell you *why* to do it. I can tell you *how* to do it. I can even tell you *what* to do. But, I can't *do it* for you. You already have 100% control and influence over the hardest person you will ever lead: yourself.

This is why you must focus so much effort on yourself. You're the key to everything you want out of life. Do you want to get promoted? Then, you must get better. Do you want to earn a bigger salary? Then, you must get better. Do you want to have a better job? Then, you must get better. Do you want to provide a better life for your family? Then, you must get better.

This principle applies to everything. If you want to be more, do more, and have more in any area in your life, you must get better.

So where do you start? You guessed it. You start with yourself. Growth doesn't just happen. You must be intentional and make it happen. The moment you start developing yourself intentionally, your results will begin to improve.

For some, it will be dramatic. Those around you will be saying, *"You have changed."* That's a great sign! It means you're taking massive action, and people are noticing. For others, it will be slow and barely noticeable from day to day. However, from year to year, the change will also be dramatic.

It doesn't matter how fast or slow you grow. What matters is that you are consistently expanding your *"circle of knowledge."* If you truly want to be a high impact leader, accomplishing things you can't even imagine right now, the one thing I can tell you to do is don't stop investing time in developing yourself.

I can tell you that authentically because I have done it. I had never studied formal leadership like this before 2008. Eight years later, I'm speaking internationally and sometimes earning more in a morning talking about what's on these pages than I previously earned in an entire year when I was working as an operator on the shop floor. I could never have imagined that. If you had told me this would happen like I'm telling you now, I would have doubted you 100%. But, I've lived the principles in this book steadily for the last eight years. Everything in my life has changed, and it has changed for the better. You can also experience a similar transformation.

I don't tell you any of this to impress you. I have no need to impress you. I tell it to you to *inspire* you. I have a great need to inspire you no matter where you are or what you're doing because I know you want more out of your career and more out of life. How do I know? You're still reading.

You may not want to be a leadership speaker, trainer, and coach like me. That was so far out into my *area of ignorance* in 2008 that it wasn't even a thought. I didn't know what I didn't know, meaning I didn't even know that was possible.

But, I know you want to be more just like I do. In your mind, you may not truly believe you can do whatever it is you want to do. I'm not asking you to do that if you have doubts. But, can you at least agree with me that *it's possible*? If it's possible and you want to make it happen, I'm providing you with a toolbox full of some of the best leadership development tools available, so you can make it happen.

Maybe, you want to be more effective where you are. It's possible. Maybe, you want to steadily climb the corporate ladder. It's possible. Maybe, you want to lead the company. It's possible. Maybe, you want to own your own business. It's possible.

Focusing on improving yourself will make you a better leader without a doubt. *Leadership starts with you.* Improving yourself is the foundation for leadership. But, the realization that *it's not about you* will act as a multiplier in relation to developing your leadership skills. The most secure leaders will always make the biggest impact.

"It is the capacity to develop and improve themselves that distinguishes leaders from followers." ~ Bennis and Nanus

7

MIRROR, MIRROR ON THE WALL

THE BEST LEADERS ARE
THE MOST SECURE OF ALL

*"No amount of personal competency can compensate
for personal insecurity." ~ Wayne Smith*

When it comes to leadership, security equals stability.
Personal growth and development is the cornerstone when it
comes to being a secure, high impact leader. Being secure
means you are not threatened by others. Once I started
growing myself as a leader and noticed I was separating myself
from the crowd, the first thing I began to realize was this:
They'll never catch up. All of a sudden, the stress went away.

When you're clearing your own path forward, you will have
complete peace of mind. Why? Because you are in total
control. When you're just running with the pack, it's every
man/woman for themselves. Insecure people accuse others of
back-stabbing, brown-nosing, sucking-up, etc. as they try to get
ahead in the traditional world of organizational politics. They
don't have a clue…remember the *area of ignorance* in chapter 1?
They don't know what they don't know.

Those are the games the insecure play. Why? They have to.
They're not growing. They're coasting. Secure leaders *eliminate*
problems. Insecure leaders *cause* problems. To better
understand secure leaders, let's look at insecure leaders.

7 Problems Insecure Leaders Cause

1. **Employee Turnover** - Insecure leaders are a major reason
    for employee turnover. Numerous research studies have

revealed the #1 reason people leave an organization is because of the relationship with their direct boss. There's nothing worse than reporting to an insecure leader. They terminate the good, strong team members, or they cause good, strong team members to quit. Either way, those that can truly help lift the organization and team are prevented from doing so by the insecure leader.

2. **Employee Disengagement** - Insecure leaders create distrust with their team members, their peers, their boss, and everyone else they interact with. It doesn't take people long to realize an insecure leader is the first to take credit for anything the team does well. They are also the first to blame the team when things don't go well. As a result, the team is indirectly trained by the insecure leader to withhold information and ideas. The team members only follow because they have to, and they only do what they have to.

3. **Lack of Communication** - Insecure leaders do not openly and freely share information, doing so would only add to their insecurity. They don't want to help their boss, peers, or team members look good in any way. They want those on their team to know only what they need to know to do their job, and unfortunately, sometimes even less. Insecure leaders are afraid their team will learn more and become an even bigger threat.

4. **Lack of Accountability** - Insecure leaders are quick to point the finger of blame at anyone other than themselves. They point fingers not only at those reporting to them, but also at those who report to other leaders, at their own peers, at their boss, and at their boss's boss (of course, behind their back where insecure leaders do most of their talking). The insecure leader's tactics cause others to waste time and energy defending themselves.

5. **Lack of Teamwork** - Insecure leaders do not value teamwork because the thought of having others share their ideas openly may reveal the leader's lack of knowledge. Insecure leaders think they should have all the answers. The insecure leader also doesn't want his/her thinking to be challenged in front of others. In their mind, someone challenging their thinking would only weaken their already weak position. As a result of the leader's insecurity, teamwork is discouraged using many different excuses, methods, and tactics.

6. **Lack of Succession Planning** - Insecure leaders do not have a plan for succession. The thought of training and developing someone to take their position goes against every fiber of their being. When asked about succession, they simply name the person on the team they think can do the best job, but they are not intentionally developing them to move up the ladder. They want to keep their team members right where they are, doing what they're doing.

7. **Low Morale** - Insecure leaders create an atmosphere of low morale. The previous six problems reveal themselves as low morale. Even if team members want to work at the organization, the insecure leader has taken away their *hope for the future* and replaced it with *anxiety about the present*. Team members come to the company hoping to be respected, to matter, to advance, and to grow. However, insecure leaders create anxiety among their team. They leverage their position in threatening ways to create and maintain an anxious tension among the team.

"Saying 'I don't know' when you don't know is a sign of good leadership. Pretending to know when you don't is a sign of insecurity. By expressing your lack of uncertainty, you give the leaders around you permission to do the same thing. You send them an important message: In this organization, it is okay not to know. It is not okay to pretend you know when you don't." ~ Andy Stanley

8

FIRST IMPRESSIONS COUNT

IS YOUR INTENTION TO SERVE
OR BE SERVED?

*"Having the tenacity to lead, and the humility to serve are
the key ingredients of Transformative Leadership."*
~ Amir Ghannad

When it comes to leadership and first impressions, others want to know three things about you: Can I trust you? Can you help me? Do I matter to you? By choosing to serve others, high impact leaders answer these questions with action.

I was a front line, blue-collar factory worker for the first 10 years of my career and spent the next 10 years in direct support of those amazing people on the front lines in the blue-collar workforce, not from an office but from the shop floor. I'm one of you.

I also served in the U.S. Marine Corps as an Infantryman and received two meritorious promotions during my four years of service. I performed well in both areas. I fit in well in both environments because real people are my kind of people. But, I still needed to work on my character.

If you really want to learn about the primary obstacle I had to overcome during my life (ME!!), then I highly recommend reading my book, *Defining Influence*. In it, I share my challenges with an extremely short temper, raising my son, working with low performers in the blue-collar factories, and not knowing what I didn't know. I also share the story of my personal growth. I don't want you to think I've always known what I'm sharing on these pages. That's not what this book is about. However, *Defining Influence* is all about that, and it's packed full of leadership lessons and principles. There's a good chance it will make you take a look in the mirror too.

I'm *not* a softy. I say this because I've heard so many in the blue-collar industry whine and moan that servant leadership is a weak way to lead.

They say, *"That stuff won't work in the blue-collar world; we're different."* Usually, the military veterans are the worst. What they say is, *"We need more command and control. People just need to do what they're told to do, and everything will run smoothly."* What they are all really saying without knowing it, because they don't know what they don't know, is *they* are too weak to lead this way. People making those and similar comments are definitely standing underneath the manager's umbrella, not the leader's umbrella.

Insecure leaders, *managers of people*, are like cancer in an organization and should be improved or removed. What is always interesting to me is this: the same people that say *"servant leadership is a weak leadership model"* prefer to work *with* a secure, servant leader instead of *for* a dictating, insecure manager. It's good enough for them, but it's not good enough for their team.

They prefer it when looking up at their boss. But, they don't want their team to see it when they look up at them. Why is that? Because becoming a high impact, servant leader takes a lot of internal work. The *"it's weak"* comments are an excuse people make because they don't want to do the character work required to transform themselves and their leadership style. Doing that work on yourself is not easy. It's hard. But, it's always worth it!

What about you? Do you prefer to work *for* a weak and insecure leader? I imagine your answer is: absolutely not. Would you like to work *with* a strong and secure leader that is exactly the opposite of an insecure leader? I imagine your answer is: absolutely. Will you be that kind of leader?

Servant leaders are strong and secure, not weak and insecure. They are the strongest and most secure among us. My hope is you're strong enough to stand with us.

There's plenty of room for you on the leadership mountain

because most leaders prefer to stand at the bottom and watch the high impact leaders do all of the climbing. Managers of people prefer to rest comfortably on their position at the base of the mountain. Why? Because it's easy. *It's much easier to be given a position by your boss because you can manage well than it is to earn respect from your team because you can lead well.*

Climbing the leadership mountain gets harder the higher you go, but the higher you climb the easier it is to lead and influence people. Going back down and helping others climb the leadership mountain is even more difficult because it's no longer about you, although it did start with you. That is servant leadership.

When a climber reaches the summit of Mt. Everest is he considered a strong climber? Absolutely! If he chooses to go back down and help others make their way to the top, does he appear even stronger? Of course, he does. No one would say someone who climbed Mt. Everest, and then chose to help others climb it, is a weak leader. That is servant leadership.

Servant leadership or high impact leadership simply means your mission is to help other people succeed. There's nothing weak about that. And, you can't do it unless you have developed your character and competency first. That takes strength. Those with weak character will rest on their position, manage their team, look out for themselves, and expect their team to serve them.

My intention in this chapter was to help you understand high impact leadership, or servant leadership as it is often referred to, is simply about helping others succeed. Do you prefer to be helped by high impact leaders that have gone before you and want to see you succeed too? High impact leadership is reserved for those with the strongest of character.

"Without a doubt, one of the most significant factors in Chick-fil-A's cultural sustainability has been its commitment to the principle of servant leadership...We recognize the tremendous responsibility not only to lead, but also to serve those we lead." ~ Dee Ann Turner

9

WHO YOU ARE MATTERS

LEAD WITH CONFIDENCE, NOT ARROGANCE

"Leaders with confidence help people. Leaders with ego hurt people because they use and abuse other people."
~ John C. Maxwell

In most organizations, people on the front lines are promoted into leadership positions because they are good at what they do. They have demonstrated *they are competent.* Their job is to come in everyday and make things happen. When they can do that effectively and repeatedly, they begin to stand out. In other words, they begin to shine.

Shiny objects get noticed, so do shiny people. There's a good chance you are one of them whether you've been promoted already or whether you want to be promoted. How do I know that? Because shiny people read leadership books.

If you haven't been promoted yet and want to be or are struggling to be promoted again, I highly recommend reading my first book in this series: *Blue-Collar Leadership®: Leading from the Front Lines.* I specifically wrote it as resource for high impact leaders to use to develop their team members on the front lines that don't have a position of authority. It's formatted just like this one. 30 chapters, three pages each. In it, I teach front line team members without a position of authority how to shine. I teach them to shine in a way that allows them to be noticed by the right people, *high impact leaders,* and how to be promoted for the right reasons, both *character* and competency.

There's something else I know from my 10 years working on the front lines: THERE ARE A LOT OF HUNGRY PEOPLE WORKING THERE.

I don't mean they want a meal. I mean they want to be more, do more, and have more. They want a raise. The really hungry ones want a raise, more responsibility, and a promotion. They want to be the boss. They work hard to prove they know what to do, how to do it, and when to do it.

Unfortunately, the hungriest among them are usually ridiculed and talked about by their peers. You may have been one of them. If so, you already know what I'm trying to explain. You also know the situation you are in when you do get the promotion and are expected to lead that same group of people.

When the hungry people can do it better than anyone else and there's an opening, they get promoted, and they're *happy* about it. That's usually how it works, best case. Worst case, no one really wants to be promoted, so the boss uses his/her authority and promotes someone who doesn't want the promotion and responsibility, so they're *not* happy about it.

One of these two scenarios happens most of the time in the blue-collar world. There is a third and fourth scenario where someone transfers from another department or is brought in from the outside. But in most cases, blue-collar managers and supervisors want someone from the area who knows how to do the job because managers are not looking for leaders, they are looking for doers.

The hungry know what to do, but do they know how to lead? Most often, the answer is no. Many are given a leadership position and told to lead because they know how to get the work done themselves, not because they know how to lead.

Most of the people on the front lines have never had any leadership development training of any kind. They are typically the most overlooked and underdeveloped members in any organization. I need your help to change this. The front lines are where most of the people usually work too, so not developing them has a huge negative impact on the organization whether the managers know it or not. The leaders definitely know it!

Most often, the people filling the front line leadership

positions are hungry, underutilized people. They may have a lot of confidence because that's what got them there. But, to be a high impact leader, they will need to add humility to the equation. *Confidence alone is never enough.*

Lack of humility may have gone unnoticed when they were only responsible for themselves. Or, it may not have mattered if their boss only valued results. But, when you start to lead others, humility *will* matter. And, it will matter a lot.

Merriam-Webster's definition of humility:

• the quality or state of not thinking you are better than other people

If literally being *"better"* than other people is what got you the position you have, it may be hard to not think you're *"better."* According to many others, I'm *"better"* than a lot of people. I've been told that my entire life. But, I don't think I'm *"better." I think I'm different.* C.S. Lewis said it best, *"Humility is not thinking less of yourself. It's thinking of yourself less."* There's a fine line between confidence and arrogance. It's called humility. Humility is a choice.

Confidence – Humility = Arrogance

If you choose to serve your team as a high impact leader, that alone will show your humility to the team. Only leaders who are truly humble will make the choice *to serve* their team. Managers of people walk through the door every day to be served by their team. High impact leaders walk through the door every day to serve their team. Which do you prefer?

"The people are just fine; it's our leadership that's lacking. When people perform poorly, most leaders are quick to blame them, perhaps even fire them right away. It takes introspection and humility to admit, 'That might be a consequence of my poor leadership.'" ~ Bob Chapman

10

WALKING THE TALK

TRUST IS A LEADER'S BEST FRIEND

"Trust is the one thing that changes everything."
~ Stephen M. R. Covey

Trust is the foundation of leadership. Since leadership is influence, trust determines the effectiveness of a high impact leader. The more trust you have, the more influence you will have. The more influence you have, the greater the impact you will have. The greater the impact, the greater the leader.

To influence someone, there must be trust in the relationship. Managers of people don't focus on building trust. They should, but they don't. If they did, that would make them a leader, not a manager. However, managers don't use influence to get people to act. They use their position, power, and authority.

Without trust, there is no authentic influence. Any influence will be purely artificial as I shared in Chapter 4. If you want to become a high impact leader, you must first learn to build trust. You must become skilled and intentionally seek to build trust into all of your relationships, especially with the people on your team. You're far better off when they *want* to help you accomplish the mission.

Do you want them to only do what they have to do? Or, do you want them to do more because they want to?

In order to build trust, you must understand this: *Intention* is the foundation of trust. Intention is all about feelings, and everybody has them. You have them. When others come near you, subconsciously and often consciously, you want to know their intent. First of all, it's about survival. Do they intend to do physical harm to you? You can usually determine their intent in this area pretty quickly. If yes, you either avoid them or prepare to defend yourself. If no, action isn't necessary.

Once you know you're physically safe, you move to your next question relative to their intent. Do they want to motivate you or manipulate you? How do you know? If their goal is to motivate you, their intention is mutual benefit. They're not only looking out for themselves, but also you. If their goal is to manipulate you, their intention is personal benefit. They're only looking out for themselves. If they do choose to help you, it'll only be because they need something from you. It's about them, not you. How do you know? You can feel it.

This is where feelings come in to play. If you feel they have your best interest in mind, you're able to move forward and begin to build trust into the relationship. If you feel you are only being used and manipulated, you're typically done with them and move on *unless* it's your boss. You *should* move on if your boss is manipulating you for their own benefit, but most people won't. What do they do? They quit performing, but stay because it's easier to do that than it is to leave.

However, those who are developing themselves have more options. They *will* move on. As a result, manipulative bosses tend to lose the best and brightest on their team because they have more options. Therefore, the boss is stuck with those who don't have options. They don't like the situation either, but their goal is not to grow and go. It's simply to make it through each day, get paid, and keep their benefits. And, what do they do day after day? Only what they have to. They are frustrated, and their boss is frustrated.

Reflect on the past chapters. If you truly feel the intent of your boss every day is to serve you with humility, do you feel motivated or manipulated to do your job? Motivated, without a doubt. You feel appreciated. You want to perform. But, if you truly feel the intent of your boss every day is to be served by you and you feel the boss thinks he/she is above you and better than you, do you feel motivated or manipulated? No doubt, you feel manipulated. How does your team feel?

I hope you see how the pieces of the high impact leadership puzzle are coming together. I hope you see how everything in this book is intentionally shared to help you develop the right intention and to build trust with other people, not just your team. I hope you see how you can apply these principles to not only serve your team better, but to also become recognized by other high impact leaders as one of them. When you apply what I'm teaching you, it's easy to become a shiny person. You will get noticed, and your team's performance will improve.

I was in Guatemala in 2013 as part of a 150 person team led by leadership guru John C. Maxwell. I've been mentored by John for many years, so it was a privilege to be there with him. Together, we all trained over 20,000 Guatemalan leaders in just three days. I want to share a story on intention, trust, and humility from one of my training classes.

On that day, I had a room full of 50 business executives. I was speaking on much of what I've covered with you so far. I had mentioned one way to build trust is to acknowledge your weaknesses with your team and let them know your intention is to improve. Wouldn't you like that from your boss? Your team would also like it from you. If you have humility, this is an easy thing to do. If you have too much pride and ego, it will be difficult. A manager of people will never choose to do it.

At the end, I was asked by one of the executives, *"Why should I tell my team my weaknesses? Wouldn't it be better if they didn't know? Telling them will make it harder for me to lead."* I said, *"Sir, you obviously have a false assumption. You assume your team doesn't already know your weaknesses."*

Do you know your boss's weaknesses? Absolutely. Did he/she have to tell you? Absolutely not. Telling your team lets them know you know your weaknesses too, and you care about improving in those areas. *If you improve*, that builds trust. *If you don't*, that creates distrust.

"A warm, trustworthy person who is also strong elicits admiration, but only after you've established trust does your strength become a gift rather than a threat."
~ Amy Cuddy

11

MOVING BEYOND COMMUNICATION

THE BEST LEADERS
INTENTIONALLY CONNECT

*"When dealing with people, you are not dealing
with creatures of logic. You are dealing with
creatures of emotion." ~ Dale Carnegie*

When you're able to build trust with your team, you move
beyond communication and begin to connect. When you
connect with your team, you're building relationships. When
you build relationships, people begin doing things to help you
succeed because they *want to*, not because they *have to*.

I'm always blown away by *"leaders"* who do not connect
with their team. If you only talk to your team members when
you need to tell them something to do or tell them something
about the mission or the job, you are not connecting. You are
simply communicating.

Managers communicate. High impact leaders connect.

Once, I was supporting a team that would meet every
morning to discuss their daily schedule before dispersing to
make things happen. I was only there a short period of time as
usual. One thing I always do intentionally to move beyond
communication and increase my influence with team members
is to go in earlier than necessary to talk with the team and get
to know them. I go in, ask some questions, make some jokes,
listen to their stories, and laugh at their jokes as they harass
each other in a fun kind of way. I get to know them.

I don't get paid to go in early. It's not always about pay.
However, it is always about connecting with the team.

I would go in early to listen to them laugh and talk every

morning. They were a great group with great intentions. Their morning meeting was always scheduled to start at the top of the hour. They were always in much earlier than necessary. Why? They were connecting with each other and enjoyed it.

Their boss was never there early and was sometimes even late. Yes, they would be looking up at the clock and rolling their eyes. I was a witness because I was there, and they trusted me because I had been connecting.

Each day at the top of the hour *or shortly after*, in comes the boss. The team went instantly silent as the door opened. The boss comes in and hands everyone a daily schedule. No hello. No how is everybody? No jokes. No laughs. The team said nothing. The boss told everyone what needed to be done. At the end, the boss asked if there were any questions. There never were any. Silence. Then, the boss would leave the room, and the team would come back to life and discuss what should have been discussed in the meeting. This was not some days, this was every day. This is very typical. I've seen it often.

This was an example of a *manager of people* in action. No leadership at all, just management of people and processes. No connection, only communication. No real influence, only the artificial influence that came with his position.

I had been in the room 15 or 20 minutes before the boss arrived. This was a good team. They cared about each other and the mission. They didn't just talk about meaningless stuff each morning. They had their *meeting before the meeting* and discussed where they had left off the previous day, what had taken place since they had left and the other shifts had worked, and they talked about what they needed to get done that day. They were leading themselves as most teams do when they work *for* a manager instead of *with* a leader.

Before the boss arrived and after the meeting, I would hear a lot of information I knew the boss needed to know and would want to know. But guess what, none of those things were ever brought up. The team didn't trust the boss. They trusted me, the outsider, and each other, but not the boss.

Because of my role as a consultant, I not only met with this team, but I also met with all levels of management regularly, all the way to the top manager. So, I would later be in a meeting with the boss and his boss. The big boss would be asking questions. Most often, the boss didn't have the answers, or worse, he would give an answer he *thought* was right to try to appear informed. However, I usually had the actual answers.

Why did I have the answers when the boss didn't? Because I had built trust with the team before work, during work, and after work by connecting with them intentionally. Managers of people do not value connecting at all because it has nothing to do with managing. To managers, connecting is a *waste* of their time. However, it has everything to do with leading. To leaders, connecting is an *investment* of their time.

Unfortunately, the boss would blame his team later for not informing him. Everyone would be pulled together for a meeting that I wasn't invited to. I usually knew what went on though because the team would tell me later. They trusted me. They knew they mattered to me. They knew my intention was to help them. They knew I was helping them shine the light on the issues that needed to be addressed.

I usually know what's going on at every level because I connect with everyone. When I'm on a team, I take responsibility for everything because I'm a high impact leader. As a result, I know the value of connection relative to my ability to accomplish the mission. I'm not there just to get paid. That's how managers operate. I'm there to make a difference. That's how high impact leaders operate.

Does your team trust you? Do you *know*, or do you *think* you know? You can't make someone trust you no matter how much authority you have. All you can do is walk the talk and choose to become a trust-worthy high impact leader. If others don't trust you, it's not their fault. It's *your* fault. *Who you are on the inside* will determine if you are trusted on the outside.

"The art of communication is the language of leadership."
~ James Humes

12

SQUINT WITH YOUR EARS

LISTEN WITH THE INTENT TO UNDERSTAND

"Authentic listening is not easy. We hear the words, but rarely do we really slow down to listen and squint with our ears to hear the emotions, fears, and underlying concerns."
~ Kevin Cashman

If connecting is so important, what's the most effective way to do it? You listen. Not with the intent to reply as managers do, but you listen with the intent to understand as high impact leaders do. When you listen to understand, you are not agreeing or disagreeing. You are simply trying to ensure you truly understand the other person.

If you want to connect quickly, squint with your ears to listen between the words for emotion, concern, fear, restraint, anger, distrust, uncertainty, etc. Let the other person know you understand by reflecting and acknowledging what you're receiving from them. Unless you've done the hard work of building trust ahead of time, this will be difficult. A high impact leader's goal is to create an atmosphere of emotional safety, built on trust, for the team members.

If you had a choice between two bosses, and one was only concerned with ensuring you understood him, and the other was concerned with first ensuring he understood you, which would you prefer to have as a boss? Which would have more influence with you? The one who wants to understand you. It's common sense right? But, is that what most bosses do? Is that what your boss does? Is that what you do?

That's definitely what high impact leaders do because they know the key to influence is to first allow yourself to be influenced.

Think about the story from the last chapter. When the boss walked into the room was his goal to first understand the team? Did he interact and ask questions at the start? No. He first told them what he wanted them to understand without knowing any of the issues they had already discussed.

He would say things that made no sense to the team because of what the reality was. But, he didn't know the reality, he didn't ask. He did what managers do. He assumed he knew all he needed to know. High impact leaders assume there's a lot they don't know but need to know.

After telling the team what he wanted them to know, he asked if there were any questions. What he was asking without asking was, *"Do you understand me?"* No one had any questions, so he assumed they understood, and he left the room thinking he had accomplished the mission.

This a perfect example of what Andy Stanley meant when he said, *"Leaders who don't listen will eventually be surrounded by people that have nothing to say."* This is exactly what was going on in the team meeting. The boss never intentionally listened to understand, so the team never had anything to say. They had plenty to say to anyone that truly had concern, wanted to help, and wanted to listen. They all talked to me non-stop. And, they had great ideas and great intentions.

When is the last time you intentionally made time to listen to and connect with each of your team members one on one? Have you ever done it? When is the last time your boss did it with you?

I worked with a client once who hired me in an effort to help the manager and the assistant manager better connect with each other. They were having some issues and the organization was suffering as a result. The facility they were managing was small with less than 20 team members on site in a building a little larger than a three bedroom house.

One day when I arrived, the manager came in wide open. She was obviously busy but slowed down enough for our session. She talked to me privately before the assistant manager arrived. I asked her about her team, specifically how she communicated with them and when. I was blown away when she said, *"I really don't get to talk with them too much unless there's a problem. I'm always too busy. Some days, I don't talk to them at all."* I couldn't believe what I was hearing.

Picture walking into the front door of the building. On the left were three or four offices with full windows, in the center a big open space for customers to sit, and to the right were several counters to provide service for the customers. There was also a drive thru and a few people working in the back area behind the counters. This was a small place.

I didn't see how it was possible for the manager of the team to walk through the door, walk into her office, and not speak to them, much less how she managed to not speak to them all day. None of them were ever more than 50 feet away from the manager's office. No wonder they were having communication issues. They were communicating when necessary. But, there was no connection between the managers and between the manager and the team.

What do you think was being communicated loud and clear to the team every day by the manager? I can tell you what she communicated to them every day without ever saying a word: YOU DON'T MATTER TO ME! She was screaming it without making a sound.

I hear managers tell me they don't have time to talk to their team members and witness team members not being talked to by their boss all the time. I'm also amazed how often I ask a manager how many people are on their team to only hear them say, *"I don't know."*

There is a lot of poor leadership in organizations today. I need your help to change that. I hope you choose to step up and become a high impact leader. You need to make a bigger difference. You can make a bigger difference.

What do your actions communicate to your team?

"The most important thing in communication is to hear what isn't being said." ~ Peter Drucker

13

LEADING BY EXAMPLE

YOU'RE ALWAYS TEACHING WHAT YOU'RE MODELING, REGARDLESS OF WHAT YOU'RE TEACHING

"Example isn't another way to teach, it's the only way to teach." ~ Albert Einstein

There's nothing worse for a team than to have their leader expect one thing from them while he/she is doing something completely different to them. Someone is always watching, so the question is not, *"Are you a role model?"* The real question is, *"What kind of role model will you be?"*

Do you want a positive, upbeat, motivated team? Then, you must be a positive, upbeat, motivated leader. A negative, demoralizing, finger pointing boss will always have a negative, demoralized, finger pointing team.

That's what managers of people do. They blame. They don't take responsibility. Their actions provide the most powerful example for their team.

I want to share what I think is one of the worst examples of poor modeling by managers of people that I see, and I have seen it a lot. High impact leaders would never do this. However, weak leaders and managers do it on a daily basis. It's just who they are, and worse, it's what they model.

I have heard front line bosses blame their boss repeatedly when the schedule changes, the hours change, or some other change comes down the pipeline from above. The leader is often more frustrated than their team by the change. Once they voice and act out their frustrations as they deliver the news of the change to the team, the team usually follows their leader's example. They moan, groan, and whine just like their boss did. Again, this is not leader behavior. This is manager behavior. Leaders of people shine. Managers of people whine.

I've been there to witness it all play out many times. The boss shows up out of nowhere. The boss you never seem to see unless there's a problem, a change, or some information needs to be passed along. The boss pulls everyone together. Once everyone is in a huddle, the boss usually begins by saying, *"I've got some bad news."*

That's not the way to motivate and inspire a team to positively accept the change. But, the boss often sets the stage for their communication by defining what they are about to say as *"bad"* news. Until that moment, it was simply news. The boss chooses to label the information as *"bad"* news. Next, the boss reinforces it to be sure everyone sees it as *"bad"* by painting a *"bad"* picture with their words. The team already knows what to expect because they've seen and heard this behavior modeled by their boss many times before.

After saying it's *"bad"* news, the boss immediately begins to tell the team who or what is to blame for the change. Often, the boss blames multiple people and multiple departments. Sometimes, they even blame their customers. Their boss's goal: Be sure the team doesn't blame them or think they had anything to do with the *"bad"* news, other than delivering it.

Next, the boss delivers the *"bad"* news to the team as they shake their heads, roll their eyes, smirk, and voice their frustrations to affirm it is *"bad"* news. Best case, the boss listens to the frustrations and smooths it all over as much as possible before leaving the area. Worst case, they simply deliver the *"bad"* news, turn around, and walk away. Regardless of when the boss leaves, it's not over.

Once the boss leaves the area, guess what the team does? They blame all those the boss blamed. But, they also blame someone new: their boss. Yes, they blame their boss too. They stand around in their huddle and blame the boss pointing fingers just as they have been trained by the boss to do when something changes. The boss has perfectly modeled for the team: When something changes, we should blame someone. There's a good chance the boss learned it from his boss.

Their morale has been lowered. Their productivity has been lowered. Their opinions of others have been lowered. And, their trust in their boss and each other has been lowered.

The example I just shared creates distrust among the team, not trust. When you talk about and blame others behind their back, you are modeling who you are on the inside to those watching from the outside. Without actually saying it, you are communicating to everyone, *"If I'll talk about and blame others behind their back, I'll do the same to you."*

A boss that blames others when there are changes, is simply a manager of people. They are not high impact leaders. High impact leaders model well developed character and accept responsibility for improving morale, increasing productivity, improving opinions of others, and building trust among their team and in their organizations. When there's a change, high impact leaders proactively deal with it in a positive manner.

Modeling is so important because who you are is who you attract. High impact leaders are able to build high impact teams because they attract team members that are like them. If you want to create a high impact team or be on a high impact team, you must become a high impact leader.

Do you want your team to listen to you? Then, you must listen to them. Do you want your team to trust you? Then, you must trust them. Do you want your team to accept and embrace change in a positive way? Then, you must accept and embrace change in a positive way. Do you prefer your team not to blame you? Then, you must not blame others.

As I've shared with you already, high impact leadership is not about you. But, it starts with you. *Who you are matters.* If you want to achieve more on the outside, you must first become more on the inside. You get better by choice, not by chance.

"We don't tend to drift into better behavior." ~ Bill Hybels

14

UNLEASHING YOUR TEAM

THE FRONT LINE DETERMINES
THE BOTTOM LINE

*"To truly get smart, you'll have to strain yourself on many
levels. You'll read more than you ever thought you would.
You'll have to think purposefully about what you've read
and digest it into nuggets of insight. You'll need to put
yourself out there, discussing these nuggets with colleagues
and be willing to debate the issues. Often, you'll have to
employ creative powers, associating unrelated facts or
examples to give new insights." ~ Tim Sanders*

If high impact leadership begins with you, but it's not about
you, what is it about? It's about you unleashing your team to
perform at a higher level. As you may have noticed, the focus
so far has been on you. That's by design, not by accident.

High impact leaders release their team while managers
suppress their team. One reason managers don't focus on
leading themselves well is because they're not focused on
leading their team at all. Their focus is on management of the
team and the processes. Your team's results are based upon
your ability to lead them. The foundation for leading them well
begins with leading yourself well.

Managers tend to focus on what they can't do instead of
what they can do. Why? Because when they can't do it,
everyone knows they can't do it, and it is a fact they can't do it,
no one expects them to do it. They are free to do nothing.

Managers also tend to shy away from the things they can
do. Why? Because when they can do it, everyone knows they
can do it, and it is a fact they can do it, they're expected to take

responsibility and do it.

High impact leaders don't focus on the things they can't do. It's a waste of time and energy because their goal is to make things happen, not watch things happen. High impact leaders don't think *"Can I?"* They think *"How can I?"*

How can you as a leader unleash your team's potential? By unleashing your own. You're off to a great start by continuing to read this book. But, if you're thinking *"Can I do or should I do what Mack's asking me to do?"* as you read the principles in each chapter, you're missing the point and are already looking for an excuse not to do it. That's a manager's way of thinking. You're not reading this book to learn how to be a manager.

But, if you're thinking, *"How can I do what Mack's asking me to do?"* as you read these pages, you're thinking like a high impact leader. From the start, *"Can I?"* places self-doubt in your mind. The easy answer is no. But, *"How can I?"* assumes there is a way, and you can do it. You just need to figure out how, and then, make it happen.

Don't miss the principle here. It applies in all situations whether you're attempting something yourself, working with a child at home, or leading your team at work.

When you're introducing anyone to change, asking them to do something new, or want them to think or act differently, don't begin your question to them with *"Can you…"* or *"Will you…"* If you do, they will instantly pick up on the fact that you're already unsure of their ability or desire to do what you're asking. Their easy answer will then be *no.* By simply adding *"How"* to the front of your questions, you will begin to change, influence, and improve the way they think.

They will instantly think you believe they can do it. So, they are more likely to try and figure out how to do it. Instead of telling them what to do as managers do, ask them thought provoking questions and allow them to figure out how to do it. Then, they will be more bought-in to the method of doing it. They will also begin to take ownership for getting the results.

At this point, you're almost halfway through the book. If you're truly gaining some new insights, truly interested in continuing to grow and develop yourself into a high impact leader, and truly want to unleash your team's potential, I want you to pause at the end of this chapter.

For those of you who are not as serious about your growth, keep reading. This exercise is not for you. But, for those who are more serious about getting to the next level, it's time to be intentional. Growth doesn't just happen. You must become intentional. It's time to invest time and effort into growing yourself. It's time to stop reading and start reflecting.

It's time to ask yourself *"How?"*

- How can I take action now?
- How can I apply what I've learned?
- How can I apply what I've learned at work?
- How can I apply what I've learned at home?

This chapter is where I make the transition and begin to focus on helping you unleash your team's potential, but it starts with helping you unleash your own. How can you unleash your own potential? By accepting this intentional growth challenge.

I would like for you to get a pen and paper or your favorite electronic device. Then, go back to the front of this book and review each chapter including this one. As you review each chapter, I want you to ask yourself one simple question related to taking action:

How can I apply what's in this chapter to make myself a more effective leader? Then, list 1 to 3 things per chapter.

Next, think about why you should do them and what will change when you do them. Finally, start doing those things!

"Praise isn't merely a reaction to a great performance; it is a cause of it. Less than a third of people report that they frequently receive praise or recognition for good work. This suggests that they did something at a level of excellence and no one praised them for it, or that they haven't performed at a level of excellence recently. Of course, neither is a good thing." ~ Marcus Buckingham

15

TWO POWERFUL THINGS

THE MIRROR AND THE WINDOW

*"You can't change what you can't change. But,
you've got to change what you can." ~ Nick Vujicic*

If you accepted my intentional growth challenge, it's a sign
of humility. You truly believe you need to change, you need to
get better, you should get better, and you want to get better.
There's a much better chance your future will be brighter than
those who chose to do the easy thing: keep reading. I predict
better relationships, better results, better pay, and a quicker
climb up the corporate ladder for you. None of that just
happens. You must make it happen. Great job!!

I love speaking at seminars and corporate training sessions
about the principles I'm about to share with you. To be highly
effective, high impact leaders must master the leadership
principles related to the mirror and the window.

The mirror and the window are tools used by both high
impact leaders and managers, although they use them in
completely opposite ways.

When it comes to responsibility, high impact leaders look in
the mirror and *accept responsibility*. Managers look out the
window and *transfer responsibility*.

Consider the intentional growth challenge from the last
chapter. If you took the challenge, you looked in the mirror
and accepted the responsibility of growing yourself
intentionally. If you didn't take the challenge, you looked out
the window and transferred the responsibility of growth to
others. The high impact leaders reading this book said to
themselves, *"This applies to me."* and did it. The managers looked

out the window and said, *"This doesn't apply to me; it applies to someone else."* and didn't do it.

This clearly illustrates the difference in mindset between high impact leaders and managers. High impact leaders knew without a doubt they were responsible for their growth and took action. Managers didn't think there was a need to grow and didn't act.

At this very moment, those with a high impact leader's mindset are agreeing with me, and those with a manager's mindset are defending themselves and making excuses for not doing it. Some of them may even be blaming me for writing this paragraph, as if it's my fault they chose not to invest in the growth and development of themselves.

This leads me to the next use of the mirror and window. When things go wrong, high impact leaders look in the mirror and *take the blame*. Managers look out the window and *transfer the blame*.

If a high impact leader's team is not performing as well as it should be, the leader looks in the mirror asking:

- How can I help?
- What am I not doing that I should be doing?
- What can I do better?
- What do I need to know that I don't know?

If a manager's team is not performing as well as it should be, the manager looks out the window saying:

- They aren't working hard enough.
- They don't do what I tell them to do.
- They don't listen.
- They don't work together as a team.

What about when things are going well? Who gets the credit for the success? High impact leaders look through the window and *give credit to others*. Managers look in the mirror and *take the credit*.

High impact leaders are happy to give the credit to others and to their team. They're already the leader. They don't need to take the credit. Humble leaders also don't want the credit.

They just want to make things happen.

Managers, on the other hand, are credit hogs. They'll jump in front of a team or a team member to take the credit when the big boss is around. It's sad. But, unfortunately, it's all too common along the front lines in the blue-collar world.

I remember working in a plant while I was in upper management on the Plant Manager's staff, serving as the Lean Manager. The CEO of our multi-billion dollar global company was coming to our plant for the first time to present a trophy we had won for our continuous improvement efforts.

We planned a tour around the plant with a stop in each department, so he could learn why we had done so well. In most plants, the Plant Manager along with the staff managers would lead this type of tour, but not at our plant.

We had an outstanding Plant Manager who was a true leader. He had a front line operator from each department work with their team to decide what they wanted to present to the CEO. Then, each of them put a flip chart in their department with that information on it. Next, we supported them as they rehearsed and prepared for the CEO's visit.

When the CEO arrived, we assembled all of the front line operators and informed him they would be leading the tour. The plant manager and all of us on his staff brought up the rear and followed them around. We didn't speak at all. It wasn't about us. We didn't achieve the results. Those hard working people on the front lines made it all happen.

We made it very obvious to those we were serving: We don't want the credit for what you have done. We don't deserve the credit. But, you do.

We leveraged the CEO's visit and gave credit to our team. Instead of creating distrust, we intentionally built trust.

"A good leader takes a little more than his share of the blame, a little less than his share of the credit."
~ Arnold Glasow

16

MAKE IT HAPPEN!

LEADERS GET RESULTS,
MANAGERS PLAN TO GET RESULTS

"The command-and-control approach is far from the most efficient way to tap people's intelligence and skills. To the contrary, I found that the more control I gave up, the more command I got." ~ Capt. D. Michael Abrashoff

When high impact leaders want to know what's happening, they go to the front lines and find out for themselves. They eliminate the middle men, get in the trenches with their team, talk to the people, and ask a lot of questions.

They don't look at a report or a computer screen. They go for a walk. They intentionally ask questions. They get their hands, and sometimes their clothes, dirty. They go see for themselves. In other words, they become fully engaged with their team and the process. Because they fully embrace the responsibility of getting results, they are not satisfied with *thinking* they know. They want to *know* they know.

Managers are quick to trust a report or a computer screen. One reason is because if it's wrong, they have an excuse. Another reason is because it's quick. Another reason is because it doesn't involve interacting with the team. The most likely reason is because it's easy. Why can a manager get away with this when a high impact leader can't? Because the manager is *planning* to get results and the leader is actually *getting* results.

I've got the perfect story to illustrate the difference between planning for results (managing) and getting results (leading).

There was a time I reported to a Plant Manager who led by report. If he wanted to know what was going on, he would hold a meeting in the conference room. The kind of meeting where everyone walks in with a report of some type and talks about what they think the problems are based on the reports. For me, these meetings were a pure waste of valuable time. Because I spent 90% or more of my time on the shop floor where the *real* problems were occurring. As a result, I knew nearly everything being said was completely inaccurate.

The meeting would lead to a list of action items most of which would never be started, much less completed. Then, the team would dismiss to go save the world. The reality: Nothing changed. Then, a few weeks later, we would do it all over again. Luckily, I reported to this manager for only a short time before he left the organization.

He was replaced by a high impact leader. The new leader walked in the door and accepted responsibility for addressing the same exact issues as the manager he had replaced. As you already know, managers and leaders do things differently. The new leader came in to get results, not plan for results as the previous manager had been doing.

Within a week or so of being on site, he gathered up those of us that reported to him. He gave gloves to those that didn't already have them. I had a well-worn pair, but most didn't have any at all. He took us all out to one of the departments that wasn't performing well. Anyone could read the reports and guess what the problems were. High impact leaders don't guess what's going on. They find out what's going on.

When we got to the department, our new leader told all of us to find a machine and have the operator train us how to operate it. He didn't just tell us to do it. He did it with us. After several hours of laughing with the operators as they taught us how to do their job, our leader gathered us and the operators together and thanked us all for participating.

I must mention one of my peers, an obvious *manager of people*, refused to participate. He stood in the aisle, arms crossed, holding his new pair of gloves. He voiced to some of us he hadn't gone to college to be a machine operator. He put on a full display of pride and ego for our team members and our new leader. After refusing to change (get onboard), he was eventually changed (replaced). The leaders were glad to see him go. The managers clearly understood it was time to change or be changed. I loved this new high impact leader!

One of the things our new leader discovered that day was which of us were leaders and which of us were managers. You can understand by now, leaders of people do not want managers of people on their team. Leaders know the damage they cause to the team and the organization is significant.

When we were done operating the machines, our new leader told us all to assemble in the conference room. Then, he stood at the white board with a marker and began to go around the room asking each of us what we had learned. As we answered, he listed it all on the board. There were all kinds of issues such as: tooling issues, safety issues, equipment issues, quality issues, maintenance issues, etc.

Once everything was documented, he looked at us and said, *"Now, go fix it all."* Then, he walked out of the room and closed the door behind himself. He knew there would be some discussions to follow. Mostly, what I heard after he left was a lot of moaning and groaning. Why? Because now the managers had to actually go do some real work, instead of talk about reports. There was a new sheriff in town, and he was a leader.

You would think everyone would want to fix the problems, but that's not what managers want to do. Managers like to talk about problems. Leaders like to fix problems. You have a choice to make every day when you walk in to work. Will you be part of the problem as managers are? Or, will you be part of the solution as leaders are? The choice is yours.

The leader I described in this story got results. He identified the leaders and turned us loose to make things happen. In just three short years under his leadership, we went from -3% gross profit margin to +35% gross profit margin. As you can see, *leaders get results* while managers are planning to get results.

> *"The secret to getting ahead is getting started."*
> *~ Mark Twain*

17

CLEARING THE PATH

LEADERS REMOVE THE OBSTACLES

"Leaders who navigate do even more than control the direction in which they and their people travel. They see the whole trip in their minds before they leave the dock. They have a vision for their destination, they understand what it will take to get there, they know who they'll need on the team to be successful, and they recognize the obstacles long before they appear on the horizon." ~ John C. Maxwell

If you were the CEO, what would you do right now to make your job better? This is one of the questions I often ask after introducing myself to front line team members. I'm sometimes amazed by the simple answers I often hear:

- Buy everybody a broom
- Add a hook here to hold my tool
- Put trash cans in all the work areas
- Go out and personally thank the people for the job they do
- Buy some tools, so I won't have to bring my own
- Add a light to my area, so I can read my gauges better

I could fill up this book with the simple answers I often get when I ask that question. What do they all have in common? They were made by people that have a manager for a boss. Anyone on a leader's team would have already had these issues addressed because the leader would have been asking *"How can I help you?"* Leaders intentionally remove obstacles which also *builds* trust and *strengthens* relationships.

49

These things appear to be insignificant when viewed through the eyes of a manager. But to a leader, the little things are the big things. Why? Leaders know when it comes to people, the little things *are* the big things.

Look back at the simple list. These are not major obstacles, or are they? They are *huge* because they stand in the way of building relationships. These little things send a message: You don't matter. It's extremely difficult to build relationships when people feel like they don't matter.

If you want to intentionally grow yourself as a high impact leader, go to everyone on your team and ask them that question the next time you go to work. You may get some wild and crazy answers. If you do, simply say, *"Realistically speaking, what would you do today to make your job better if you were the CEO? The reason I'm asking is because I want to see if I can help you make it happen."*

Then, be a leader and make it happen. If you can't for some reason, go back to the person and explain what you did and why it's not going to happen. Then, find another way to help. That will help you sustain trust. If you simply avoid them, you will pay a double trust tax. One for not addressing the issue and another for not following up with them.

As a high impact leader, you will also be aware of obstacles you can remove or eliminate for your team. The team may not even be aware you have the ability to remove them. They may have gotten used to working around them or battling through them every time they do a certain job, work on a certain part, or work in a certain area.

These *"hidden"* obstacles will only be removed by a high impact leader who takes responsibility for doing more than is required and doing it before it's required. High impact leaders proactively search for obstacles to remove. That's why they're *often* engaged with their team and always asking questions. They are looking for ways to help their team get better. Leaders understand when the team gets better results the leader begins to shine a little brighter too. It's a win-win situation.

However, when managers discover these *"hidden"* obstacles,

they react in a different way. They hope no one notices, especially their boss. If their boss notices, they're afraid they'll be told to remove the obstacle. They don't want more work getting in between them and pay day. Managers are not problem solvers. They are problem avoiders, and they are really good at it too. I've seen some of the best in action.

I remember once when I was a front line machine operator. I reported to a team leader who was a manager of people. If you look up *"manager of people"* in the dictionary, I'm sure you would find a picture of this guy.

He often badmouthed us for trying to make our jobs easier. He would call us lazy in an effort to get us to quit offering up process improvements. He always said we were creating extra work for him. But the big boss wanted our ideas and suggestions, so this guy was not only not helping us remove the obstacles, *he* was an obstacle. Managers of people are always obstacles. Leaders of people are obstacle removers.

The thing I remember most about that team leader was what he would say to us when we offered him a suggestion for an improvement and asked him, *"What do you think?"* He always offered the same response, *"They don't pay me to think."* I'm serious. This was our *"leader."* Needless to say, we didn't make a lot of improvements beyond what we could do without his help.

High impact leaders always have influence beyond their own area of direct responsibility. Therefore, they can often eliminate an obstacle simply by asking someone else to do it or by asking someone else to help.

If you're a high impact leader, removing obstacles is not your job. It's your responsibility. *Will you help your team help you?*

"When you are an individual contributor, you try to have all the answers. When you are a leader, your job is to have all the questions." ~ Jack Welch

18

LEADING WITH QUESTIONS

THE BEST LEADERS
ASK THE MOST QUESTIONS

"As we look ahead into the next century, leaders will be those who empower others." ~ Bill Gates

There's a tremendous amount of power in a question. High impact leaders leverage this power for many reasons by asking their team A LOT of questions.

The primary motive of managers of people is to make decisions. If they're asking a question, it is simply to gather only enough information to be used in their decision-making process. Beyond gathering information, managers don't ask questions and don't want unsolicited advice.

Insecure leaders (managers) don't want it to appear as though they don't have all the answers. So, they don't ask a lot of questions. Insecure leaders don't want someone else to get credit for an idea. So, they don't ask a lot of questions. Insecure leaders don't want too many people involved in a solution because they're unable to effectively lead a group discussion. So, they don't ask a lot of questions. Insecure leaders don't want others to gain influence. So, they don't ask a lot of questions.

The primary motive of high impact leaders is to facilitate decision-making among their team members. They don't want to make all the decisions. They do want to grow and develop every member on their team and understand asking questions is one of the most effective ways to do just that. Here are seven reasons to ask effective, thought provoking questions.

7 Reasons to Ask Your Team Questions

1. **To show them respect.** Asking questions demonstrates respect. It lets them know they matter and shows their opinions are valued and appreciated. It builds trust into the relationship. It allows the leader to model teamwork.

2. **To transfer influence to them.** Asking questions allows them to influence the leader. It allows them to feel understood which creates more buy-in. When the team feels understood, they are more likely to support the path forward.

3. **To give them a voice.** Asking questions allows the team to be involved in finding the solution. It allows them to have ownership in the process and the decision.

4. **To learn how they think.** Asking questions is a valuable tool because it allows the leader to learn how each individual thinks. It allows the leader to learn which team members are ready and want to lead.

5. **To engage them in the process.** Asking questions allows the leader to share the responsibility and engage the team. It gets team members involved who may otherwise keep their opinions to themselves. It empowers the team to act instead of being acted upon.

6. **To uncover hidden concerns.** Asking questions allows team members to express concerns that may have otherwise remained unknown. It allows the leader to confirm the facts and minimize the rumors that spread so quickly along the front lines.

7. **To develop a better solution.** Asking questions creates a synergistic environment which allows the leader to think with many minds instead of just one. It helps all team members to realize that none of them is as smart as all of them.

Questions allow you to steer the team as you grow and develop them. By asking the right questions at the right time in a group discussion, you can create teamwork and validate it right on the spot. As you ask questions and the team develops solutions, always be sure to show gratitude to them as a team. Don't fall into the manager's trap of acknowledging only the person that comes up with the final solution. There are usually many thoughts that have been bounced around that created *"group think,"* so acknowledge the group as a whole.

Questions also allow you to grow yourself as a leader. The better your questions are, the better the team's answers will be. Nguib Mahfouz expressed it this way, *"You can tell whether a man is clever by his answers. You can tell whether a man is wise by his questions."*

Great questions lead to great answers.

Don't miss the point. The power of the question is multiplied by your ability to listen and ask an impactful follow up question that allows the other person to dig a little deeper for a better answer or a totally different answer. It's the question after the question that often provides the best answer.

If you're not getting the answers you want, it's most likely because you're not asking the right questions. Focus on open ended questions. Avoid asking questions that allow others to answer with a simple yes or no. Make them think.

You will know you are in the high impact leader zone when you begin to answer questions from your team members with another question. When team members ask a manager a question, they get an answer. But when they ask a high impact leader a question, they get a question. It's a leader's job to grow their team. When we give them answers, we are not growing them. We are showing them. Be intentional. Answer more questions with questions. Questions make people think.

"Some people assume we stumble onto our success, but the path of discovery is paved with interesting questions."
~ Bryan Cioffi

19

HOW HIGH WILL YOU CLIMB?

DEVELOP YOURSELF WITH THE INTENTION OF DEVELOPING OTHERS

"Your capacity to grow determines your capacity to lead."
~ Mark Miller

I've shared many principles that will help you climb to the top of the leadership mountain. So far, I've been focused on getting you to the top by helping you become a *highly effective* leader of yourself and your team. But remember, getting to the top will make you a great leader, but it will not make you a high impact leader.

If you want to become a high impact leader, you must go back down and help others climb their way to the top effectively and efficiently. Great leaders treat their teams with respect, build great relationships, value them, and help them get great results, but they *seldom* intentionally do more than is *required* to develop their team.

Managers of people don't develop their team members because they are insecure. They feel threatened by anyone and everyone for various reasons. Actually, their goal is to make sure everyone stays in their place, doesn't threaten them, and learns to do their job. When they must fill a position, their biggest objective is to find someone that will stay in the position and not move upward or onward.

Great leaders are very secure. However, they also don't develop their team members. These leaders are unwilling to pay the additional price of developing themselves beyond what is required to do their job. I've met many great leaders who are content with who they are and what they're doing.

They are not growth oriented. They are goal oriented. And unfortunately, they have reached their goal. It may be a certain salary or a certain position. Whatever it is, they no longer want to grow. They are content to coast. But, what are they leaving on the table?

Some are team leaders. Some are supervisors. Some are managers. Some are directors. Some are vice-presidents. Some are presidents. Some are CEOs. Some are business owners. They are everywhere. The world needs them to step up, but they don't have any desire to step up. They're content.

Are you one of them? Are you going to settle for success? Success is about you. It's about reaching the top of the mountain. But, there's something beyond success. It's what you can only find if you choose to go back down the mountain. I'm talking about significance. Significance is about helping others become successful.

Position and title don't have anything to do with what I'm asking you to consider. At this point, I want to know if you're one of those special leaders. I want to know if you have the desire to grow beyond what is required of you and become a high impact leader.

You can become a great, successful leader by developing yourself at work. But to truly become an exceptional high impact leader, you must choose to work on developing yourself when you're not at work. Very few leaders are willing to make this kind of sacrifice.

Until I left the corporate world, I was just another great leader making things happen. I didn't know what I didn't know about leadership or what I was leaving on the table.

I got great results. The teams I led got great results. They liked me, and I liked them. That's great leadership. I did an exceptional job at doing what was expected at work. However, when I got off work, I didn't do anything to develop myself.

Why should I? I had it made. Nice cars. Nice home. Nice vacations. Nice wife. Nice life. That was my goal at the time, and I had reached that goal. Success!

For high impact leaders, success is truly the starting point.

For all other leaders, success is the stopping point. Something happened the same year I left the corporate world. I was exposed to professional leadership content like you're reading in this book. As a result, I started to look in the mirror. I started to become growth oriented instead of goal oriented.

I began to understand I could make a much bigger impact on the lives of others. I decided I wanted to become a high impact leader. I hope you do too.

For me, that meant giving up a lot of things that were wasting my time. I gave up toxic people. They were not toxic when I was successful. I actually called them friends at that time. As I began to grow, I realized they weren't interested. I quickly began to see they were more interested in holding me back instead of encouraging me to grow.

I quickly learned the only time I had to grow myself into a high impact leader was between the time I got off work and the time I went back to work, between 5pm and 7am weekdays and on my weekends off. That's right. I had to give up some of my personal time. But, that's a lower level leader's way of thinking. I saw it that way in the beginning too.

However, I quickly figured out I wasn't actually giving up my personal time. I was simply utilizing it better. Instead of wasting my time on meaningless activities, I began investing my time in my own personal development. I started reading. I hated to read then, and I still do. But, I've discovered I like to learn more than I hate to read. So, I read leadership books every day. I also got into leadership audios, videos, and started investing my own money to attend leadership seminars.

My results since then have been amazing. My life is on a completely different level now. I've not only increased my earning potential to figures I could never have imagined in the past, but I've also helped many others do it. *I hope you're next!*

Do you have what it takes to be a high impact leader?

"If you work hard on your job you can make a living, but if you work hard on yourself you can make a fortune."
~ Jim Rohn

20

MOTIVATION IS NEVER ENOUGH

MOTIVATION COMES FROM THE OUTSIDE, BUT INSPIRATION COMES FROM THE INSIDE

"Every once in a while I will hear someone in leadership complain about the performance or competency of the people around him...We must never forget that the people who follow us are exactly where we have led them."
~ Andy Stanley

How is your team doing? Where have you led your team?

When you look at them, it's like looking in the mirror and seeing yourself. What you see when you look at your team is a reflection of how you're doing as their leader. Their performance reflects your ability to motivate and inspire them. Your ability to lead is reflected in your team's willingness to follow you and their desire to achieve results.

Do they trust you? If not, where are you failing them? Do they respect you? If not, where are you failing them? Do they work well together? If not, where are you failing them? Are they motivated to make things happen? If not, where are you failing them? Do they solve problems on their own? If not, where are you failing them? Do they support you? If not, where are you failing them? Do they embrace change? If not, where are you failing them? Are they growing and excited about their future? If not, where are you failing them?

If you're going to be a high impact leader, having a high impact team is your responsibility. It doesn't matter if you inherited the team or you hand-picked the team. If you're going to be a high impact leader, you must grow and develop your team. Where do you start? Wherever they are.

Whenever I hear someone moaning and groaning about their team or a team member, I'll usually ask, *"What leadership book are you reading?"* The answer is most often, *"I'm not reading."* Then I follow up with, *"What's the last leadership book you've read?"* Most often, the answer is, *"I haven't read any."* Or, they'll rattle off some book they read years ago, but they can't tell me anything about it.

Weak leaders blame their team members when their ability to lead themselves is obviously the problem. Why don't these weak leaders develop themselves? It's simple. They are not inspired from within to lead themselves well. It's also usually a sign of weak leadership all the way to the top of their organization. If there was a high impact leader at the top, everyone would be growing and developing.

Leadership problems at the bottom can always be traced back to a leadership problem at the top. However, high impact leaders don't use that excuse. As I've mentioned, we are fully capable of developing ourselves and are absolutely responsible for doing so. If you get some help from above, great. If not, you must still make it happen. If you don't, you are only holding yourself back while transferring the blame to others.

If you read this book and get fired up and excited about what you can make happen, that's great! That means I have motivated you. Motivation comes from the outside. However, motivation is never enough. To change your results, you must take action. Taking action requires something beyond motivation.

Taking action requires inspiration. Inspiration comes from the inside. If you read this book and do something different as a result, I have done more than motivate you. I have inspired you. It's no longer about me, it's about you. But, it did start with me. I chose to write this book with the intention of inspiring others to become better leaders and better people. However, if you do that, you deserve the credit, not me. It's about you.

No one will ever make a single choice for you. You must make all of those by yourself, so you deserve the credit for how well your life is going or not going.

If you truly want to motivate and inspire someone to take action, help them look good because that will make them feel good. This entire book is about me helping you look good. I want to help you shine. The more you shine, the more you will be inspired to continue your growth as a leader. Also, the higher you climb up the leadership mountain, the better the view gets and the better you will feel.

Inspiration or self-motivation comes from the inside, so it starts with feelings. If you won't motivate yourself to act, you can't inspire others to act. Unmotivated leaders will never motivate their teams. If you can't motivate your team, you're not motivated yourself. That's *your* problem, not their problem.

I've seen countless unmotivated leaders come into my classes when I'm conducting onsite corporate leadership training. They come in all the same. But, they don't all leave the same. Some of them leave motivated from within (inspired). Why do some leave inspired while the others leave feeling the same way they came in? What's different? I can tell you. It's BS! No, not that BS.

It's their *"belief system."* Some believe what they're hearing is true. I was one of those people. When I was first exposed to leadership content like this, I told myself, *"I believe this is true. I believe if I do these things I will be a better leader. I believe if I do these things my life will get better. I believe I will start applying what I'm learning."* Today, eight years later, I have now proven it to be true. But initially, I simply believed it was true.

However, some attend my classes or read my books and tell themselves, *"This worked for him, but it won't for me. Mack doesn't know me. He just thinks he does. This stuff will never work. There's no need for me to try."* They don't do it. So, it doesn't work. But, it would have worked. If you're having doubts, don't. Just do it. Keep doing it and help others do it.

"You'll never get dumber by making someone else smarter."
~ Stanley Marcus Jr.

21

ABUNDANCE ALLOWS YOU TO ACCELERATE

BE A RIVER, NOT A RESERVOIR

"A candle loses nothing when it lights another candle."
~ Thomas Jefferson

In all my years of working on the front lines in various blue-collar industries, I've met and worked with many knowledge hoarders. They make it painful for those who are trying to make things happen. And, they make it extremely painful for those who are trying to learn more and contribute more.

They want to be seen as *"special"* by those they work with and the leaders they report to. They think this makes them more valuable, but nothing could be farther from the truth when seen through the eyes of a high impact leader. When it comes to knowledge, high impact leaders are rivers. Whatever they learn flows right through them and into someone else. They want others to know what they know. They know the more others know, the faster they will go and the faster the team will grow. High impact leaders are very intentional about sharing knowledge and teaching others how to do what they do.

Because they are secure leaders, no one's knowledge threatens them. It actually strengthens them. High impact leaders are focused on developing a high impact team. They also want to model knowledge sharing and succession planning. When the team performs well in their absence, they know this is a sign they are being led well. High impact teams don't skip a beat when their leader is absent.

Managers of people do not function as rivers, but instead are like reservoirs. They are intent on collecting knowledge. They don't want it to pass through them into others. They think the more they know, relative to others, the better off they are. This is natural for them since they are prideful and self-centered. They aren't focused on helping others grow and develop. Their focus is actually on minimizing others.

Since managers are insecure, they are threatened by anyone with shared knowledge or more knowledge. Managers are also not focused on team development. They simply want their team members to know what they need to know to do their job. Anyone that learns anything beyond what is required is seen as a threat. Managers of people actually want things to fall apart in their absence because they think it makes them look important and needed.

Managers want to be needed. High impact leaders want to be succeeded.

Which leader is more valuable to an organization? One that shares knowledge, or one that hoards it? I'll ask you a few sets of questions and let you decide for yourself.

Assume you are the boss and someone is going to be promoted and/or receive a raise. You can only offer this to one person. However, you have two top notch "A" players on your team. There's really only one difference between them.

One of them is a knowledge hoarder, self-centered, and loves being the hero. She is very skilled in certain areas but has been on the team for years without any concern for teaching others what she knows. She actually doesn't want others to know what she knows. When she is not at work, the team pays the price because there are some things only she can do.

The other person teaches everyone everything she knows. She does it without being asked. When she learns something new, she quickly passes it on to the rest of the team. She wants to be sure if she's not at work, the show will still go on without skipping a beat. She is team-centered, not self-centered.

You're the boss. Which one of them is more valuable to

you? Which one of them gets the promotion/raise? The answer is obvious. The one willing to train and develop others by sharing her knowledge and skills.

Now, consider another scenario. Assume there's been a business downturn, and you must let one of them go. Which will it be? There's no doubt the person that shares her knowledge and skills is the one you will want to keep on the team. She is adding much more value to you, the team, and the organization. The knowledge hoarder will be let go.

Once when I was teaching this, someone in the class got excited to share a real-life example. He was a setup man responsible for machine changeovers on the shop floor.

He proceeded to tell us when he was a machine operator and wanted to get promoted to setup man, the setup man in his area wouldn't teach him how to setup the machine. So, he decided to make a small bet that he could do it faster although he didn't really know how. As he waited his turn, he had the privilege of watching the other guy do the setup. He was learning by watching. He told the class he repeated this periodically until he had actually learned to setup the machine. Eventually, he was promoted setup man. He was very clever! The setup man was very insecure.

As a high impact leader, you want to help your peers be better leaders and team players. You also want to help your team be better team players. Share as much knowledge as possible with them and encourage them to do the same. Share knowledge even when they're not required to know what you're sharing. Sharing knowledge builds trust and increases your influence with your team and your peers.

It sends this message, *"I want to help you get better and be better. I'm looking out for you. You matter."* If you're growing and developing yourself, no one is a threat. *Make it happen!*

"Leadership is an ability and responsibility for all. Our definition of leadership is the ability to make those around you better and more productive." ~ Jack Clark

22

SUPERCHARGE YOUR TEAM

FOCUS ON CHARACTER FIRST
AND COMPETENCY SECOND

*"Do not tolerate brilliant jerks.
The cost to teamwork is too high." ~ Reed Hastings*

Supercharging teams is what I love to do! With over 11,000 hours of leading cross-functional teams through change and transformation, I've learned how to take a team of strangers, often who don't know me or each other, and achieve amazing results in just five short days.

Working with these teams is where I truly learned to lead and apply the leadership principles I'm so passionate about.

You must understand, often they didn't like me because I was an outsider. Often, they didn't like me because they didn't like the last consultant. Often, they didn't like change. Often, they didn't want to change. Often, they didn't like their boss. Often, they didn't like each other. Often, they didn't want to be on the team. Often, they had been there 20 years, and I had been there 20 minutes. All of these challenges were happening at the same time. I loved leading these teams.

Imagine that's your team, and you get a new one every week just like it. By the way, there's one catch. If you can't get them to work together and achieve amazing results within five days, you're fired. The team simply goes back to work and isn't held responsible. You carry the full responsibility of failure alone. However, there's another catch. If there is success, the team gets all the credit as you stand in the back of the room on Friday while they all stand at the front of the room and share with the executives what *they* were able to accomplish as a team.

There are very few leaders that can lead the team I've just described. Managers of people don't stand a chance. I've seen them try. It's really ugly to watch. High impact leaders are the only leaders capable of leading teams like this successfully.

I learned how to quickly supercharge the teams I led. How did I do it? I always started by focusing on character, not only theirs, but also mine. I applied everything in this book and much more. I had to learn to do it quickly. Five days isn't a lot of time to connect, build trust, develop relationships, develop people, teach them how to analyze the process, allow them to study the area and develop a plan, allow them to execute the plan and make changes, allow them to validate the results, allow them to create a presentation, and finally allow them to present their achievements to the executives and other leaders.

Most often, these teams had no experience in doing what they were expected to do. The only one that knew what to do was me, but I wasn't going to do it. I was the leader, not the doer. They were being taught to do it while they were doing it.

I remember one team improved output per person per hour 376% in one week. Another team reduced changeover/setup time from 108 minutes down to 17 minutes in one week.

I never had a bad week or a bad team. I'm not special. However, I am intentional. I intentionally and methodically applied the character-based principles of influence (leadership). These principles *are* special. They apply to all people in all situations. Not sometime. Every time.

What did I really do to make it all happen? I dedicated most, if not all, of the first day to leadership development. I didn't care who was in the room, what their title was or wasn't, and I didn't care what the mission was. I wanted to get everyone on the same page thinking the same way. I call it *"priming the pump."*

I was helping them look in the mirror and understand why it was important to *their* success for the *team* to be successful. I helped them understand *why* and *how* they should work together. I helped them understand their success was important to me. I made sure they trusted me and knew they would get all the credit for the team's success. I helped them begin to think like high impact leaders.

Your success depends on your team's success. I want to help you be more successful. How? By helping you help your team be more successful. I intentionally made this book the second in this series because I wanted to be sure I had the first one ready for you to use to grow your team. I want to help you help your team begin to think like high impact leaders while they are still on the front lines.

I wrote *Blue-Collar Leadership®: Leading from the Front Lines* specifically for leaders to use to develop their teams. You can learn about it and even download the first five chapters for free at www.BlueCollarLeadership.com. If you truly want to be a high impact leader and build a high impact team, I highly advise you to order it now since you are almost finished with this one. *You* will also *learn* a lot from it, and you will see how beneficial it will be for your team.

I wrote it in the same format as this book. 30 easy to read, three page chapters. Some high impact leaders have purchased a copy for each of their team members. The most effective leaders not only purchase it for their team members, but also lead them through a 30 day book study, one three page chapter at a time.

The *best* teams read each chapter together with each person underlining their key points. Then, the leader briefly discusses his/her key takeaway. Next, each team member briefly discusses their key takeaway. Then, everyone is dismissed.

This is a powerful learning model for developing your team and building relationships. We learn more subconsciously listening to others speak about what they learned than we do by listening to someone tell us what we should have learned.

"The ability to mobilize the skills and competencies of the people around us has a bigger impact on our performance than does the amount of experience we have." ~ Liz Wiseman

23

EVERYBODY MATTERS

THERE IS POTENTIAL IN EVERYONE

*"Treat a man as he appears to be and you make him worse.
But treat a man as if he already were what he potentially
could be, and you make him what he should be."*
~ Johann Wolfgang von Goethe

On some of the teams I've led, I've had a president sitting next to a forklift driver, a CFO sitting next to a welder, an engineer sitting next to a warehouse clerk, a supervisor sitting next to a director, or an accountant sitting next to a machine operator. I prefer to teach leadership without walls and barriers. Treating people as people and ignoring titles and positions.

Managers of people don't like my approach because they want to be with their peers when they're growing and learning. Being taught the same thing as those they lead causes *insecure* leaders to feel inferior. In their mind, they are the boss, so they are supposed to *appear* superior. They don't want to appear to be learning the same material as those on the front lines. They often want a *"special"* class for those only at their level.

High impact leaders love my approach because they get to meet the people, build relationships, connect, and model humility for everyone in the room. They also know leadership principles are universal and apply to everyone. So they ask, *"Why shouldn't we all grow and learn together?"* It's a win-win and a very effective use of time in the mind of any high impact leader. They also get to ask a lot of questions.

Managers tend to think *they* matter most. It's obvious to all. They are not concerned with the potential of others because they're not focused on developing their team. They won't lead their team through the book study I mentioned because doing so goes against every part of their being.

High impact leaders know *everyone* matters equally. It's also obvious to all. They are always trying to find ways to unleash their team's potential. They have been waiting for a resource like *Blue-Collar Leadership®: Leading from the Front Lines*. They have already ordered it and are excited about introducing it to their team members and their organization.

High impact leaders think abundance, be a river, grow and develop others, there is plenty of success for everyone. Their focus is on others. Managers of people think scarcity, be a reservoir, don't develop others, there is only so much success to be had. Their focus is on themselves.

What message will you send to your team when you make each of them feel like they matter? Will their morale go up or down? Will trust increase or decrease? Will your influence with them go up or down? Will they work better together? Will they feel inspired to be more and do more?

If you intentionally apply the principles in this book, your team will feel like they matter because you will be showing them they matter with your actions, not your words. They will feel encouraged, empowered, and engaged. They will feel like they have a leader instead of a manager. They will trust you more and want to help you succeed more.

Assume for a moment when you get to work each day there are two doors. Everything behind each door is the same except the boss. Behind one door is a boss that makes you feel like you matter. Behind the other door is a boss that makes you feel like you don't matter. Which door would you walk through every day?

When you begin to intentionally develop your team, they will feel you care for them. They will feel like you want something better for them. Does your boss intentionally develop you? If so, how does it make you feel? If not, how does it make you feel? What would your team say if I asked each of them? Does it matter? Should it matter?

Growing and developing your team is not the only way to show them they matter. It's a powerful way, but only one way.

7 Simple Ways to Make Everybody Matter

1. Talk to them regularly, especially when there's no reason to do so.
2. Give them special assignments where they can be successful and get noticed.
3. Ask their opinion about things not directly related to them or their job.
4. Ask them what their dreams are and what they would like to do in the future.
5. Find a way to help them shine.
6. Help them network by introducing them to other leaders in the organization.
7. Sincerely and regularly thank them for their contribution to the team's success, your success, and the organization's success.

As you can see, making someone feel like they matter isn't hard. If you want to do it, you'll find a way. It's easy if you truly care, and you become intentional about doing it. The more you get to know your team, the easier it will be.

Look at the list above. Is your boss doing those things? If so, great! If not, what would change if he/she did? Would your relationship be better or worse? Would you feel better or worse? Would it make you feel like you matter?

If I showed this list to each of your team members, what would they say when I asked them the questions I just asked you? Would they feel you are a manager or a leader?

If a member on your team doesn't feel like they matter, it's because they don't matter. It's that simple.

"If we lose sight of people, we lose sight of the very purpose of leadership." ~ Tony Dungy

24

BELIEVE IN YOUR TEAM

THEY NEED TO FEEL IT, NOT HEAR IT

"The very best leaders make us feel as if we are in control."
~ Jimmy Collins

Do you believe in your team? I mean, really believe in them as people, not as producers of results and profits. Or, is your belief in them based on certain conditions being met? For most, the answer to this question is an easy yes. Yes, certain conditions must be met before I can believe in someone.

I saw a great TEDx video on YouTube a few months ago by Joshua Encarnacion. He was speaking about belief, and he had some really great and profound things to say on the subject. As I listened to him, I found it easy to agree with him because I was already aligned with what he was teaching.

Joshua explained if you look up the word *"belief"* in the dictionary, you'll discover words like trust, faith, and confidence are used to define it. He went on to say believing in others this way is selfish and requires judgment. He proposed we should redefine the way we believe in people.

He said we should redefine belief in people as encouragement, empowerment, and engagement. He made the point that believing in people this way is selfless and doesn't require judgment. I really liked what he had to say, so I set up a call with the young man.

We spoke for nearly an hour. I learned his passion for what he was talking about came from his life. He had made a few mistakes, but someone had believed in him and expressed it to him as encouragement, empowerment, and engagement. Instead of judging him for his mistakes, they simply continued to believe in him. As a result, he was inspired, started making better decisions, and recovered from his mistakes. He also was inspired to teach others what the experience had taught him about believing in others.

After watching the full video and talking with Joshua, I was fully convinced I had been believing in people like this for some time. It's one of the things that has allowed me to be so effective when leading teams.

Those on the teams knew I believed in them because they could feel it. I was basically forced into believing in them as Joshua had described because I didn't know them. They were strangers. I couldn't have trust, faith, and confidence in them. That would have required me to know them in advance. Since I didn't know them, I couldn't judge them.

So, I did exactly what Joshua explained in the video. I encouraged them. I empowered them. I engaged them. In other words, I *unleashed* them. The result: they worked together, trusted me, and achieved amazing results.

This was years before I had seen the video, but what he described is a principle. Principles are timeless. He didn't invent the principle. He just defined it and revealed it to his audience in a meaningful way. When he did, he nailed it!

I'm asking you to believe in your team members in this way. It will be a little more difficult because you already know them. You may tend to be selfish and judge them. However, everything in this book will help you encourage, empower, and engage your team. That's exactly what I'm trying to do for you on these pages too. I want to help you unleash your potential.

Truett Cathy, Founder of Chick-fil-A, had this to say about encouragement, *"How do you know if someone needs encouragement? If they're breathing they need encouragement."* This entire book is ultimately about encouraging you to encourage your team. We all need encouragement. And, it won't cost you a penny to give encouragement to someone else.

In my book, *10 Values of High Impact Leaders*, one of the chapters covers *The Value of Delegation*. Learning and applying *The 5 Levels of High Impact Delegation* is one way high impact leaders empower their teams. Delegation 101: Delegating *"what to do"* makes you responsible. Delegating *"what to accomplish"* allows others to become responsible.

Outline of *The 5 Levels of High Impact Delegation:*

Level 1: Wait for Directions – Don't do anything until I tell you. You have no responsibility. I'll do all the thinking.

Level 2: Ask, *"What's Next?"* – The only responsibility you have is asking what to do next. I'll still do all the thinking.

Level 3: Recommend a Course of Action – At this level, something powerful happens, you must start thinking.

Level 4: Do It and Report Immediately – You've done all the thinking and taken action. You are fully responsible.

Level 5: Do It and Report Routinely – You are fully trusted to think and act on your own.

When you fully understand how to delegate and empower your team, you will have an engaged team. If you think delegating simply means telling someone what to do, you're already a pro at Level 1. Managers delegate at Levels 1 & 2.

High impact leaders are on a mission of empowerment and engagement and always delegate at Level 3 or above. Why? That's where all of their team's growth happens because they do most, if not all, of the thinking at those levels. At Levels 1 & 2, the boss is required to do all of the thinking.

If you want to unleash your team's potential, they must feel your belief in them. Learning, teaching, and applying *The 5 Levels of High Impact Delegation* will help you do just that.

I believe in you. Do you believe in your team?

"It is a big step in your development when you come to realize that other people can help you do a better job than you could do alone." ~ Andrew Carnegie

25

FOCUS ON YOUR LEADERS

WHEN YOU LEAD LEADERS, YOU ALSO LEAD THEIR FOLLOWERS

"There is something more scarce than ability.
It is the ability to recognize ability." ~ Robert Half

You're busy! There's only so much of you to go around, so where do you invest your time and energy when it comes to your team? Unfortunately, most leaders tend to be reactive and focus on their low performers. However, high impact leaders *are proactive* and focus on their top performers.

Managers of people focus on the low performers. Managers like to be in charge. They like to control everything. They like to flex their positional muscle of authority. As a result, they do what comes naturally. They look for those who are not following orders or performing as they think they should be and spend a lot of time and energy trying to get them to *"get with the program."*

High impact leaders do exactly the opposite. They focus heavily on their top performers. They also do what comes naturally to them: Work where they have the most influence. They like to influence people who are making things happen because those people have influence with others on the team that will help them make things happen.

I always tell leaders to invest 80% of their time on their top leaders, 15% with those in the middle of the pack, and 5% with their lowest performers.

Most managers do exactly the opposite. They focus non-stop on their low performers. These people are low performers because that's who they are. They don't want to be better. You don't want to forget about them. However, you don't want to give them too much of your valuable time and energy. Why? Because it will be wasted. They don't want to change. They also don't have much, if any, positive influence.

You and your team will be much more productive when you *invest* your time instead of *waste* your time.

Your top performers are hungry. They want to do more. They want to learn more. They want to help more. When you invest your time with them, you get an ROI, *return on investment*. In other words, you get better results. Your influence also doesn't stop with them because they are leaders (people with positive influence). Remember, leadership is not about position or title. Leadership is about influence.

Your top performers also live among the team. They will take what you give them and multiply it. They are among the other team members all the time and have the most influence with them. They have developed strong relationships with the other team members that are also performing.

Every team has a formal leader: the boss. Every team also has an informal leader: the team member with the most influence. This team member often does far more *leading* of the team than the boss does. When you invest your time building a relationship, growing, developing, and connecting with this informal leader, you will *multiply* your efforts. Why? Because the informal leader will pass it on to their followers.

When you directly lead leaders, you are indirectly leading their followers.

You are the perfect example. You're still reading this book. You're a leader and want to become a better leader. Those that want to continue managing put it down a long time ago, unless someone required them to read it as part of a book study. But, I'm still influencing you. As you learn, grow, and apply the leadership principles I'm teaching you, I will be able to positively influence your team and your family through you.

Every book I write allows me to directly influence many leaders. When that happens, I'll also be able to indirectly influence all those they formally lead at work and all those they informally influence at work and at home. It doesn't end there because some of those people are leaders which means they have followers too. As I influence you and you influence others, some of those people will also influence others.

When you positively influence influencers, you're maximizing your efforts to make a bigger difference at work, at home, in your community, your country, and ultimately in the world. As I wrote many pages ago, *leadership starts with you, but it's not about you.* I'm sure you can see the bigger picture now.

When you focus on your leaders, you get better, your team gets better, and the organization gets better. Everyone wins. You become a more shiny person, and the leaders reporting to you become more shiny. And ultimately, your team becomes more shiny. Remember, shiny things get noticed.

You will be more likely to get raises and promotions. Those on your team will be more likely to get raises and promotions. People will notice that wherever you go, you make things happen with people that want to make things happen. You will get results. People that get results always get noticed.

The key is getting results based on *positive* influence as a high impact leader. If a manager of people gets outstanding results because of his/her ability to control and manipulate their team, they still do not gain influence with the high impact leaders, only the other managers above them will relate to and value their efforts. High impact leaders care about character first and results second. They want both!

As you begin to apply what you've learned in this book, don't focus on those that aren't on board. Focus on those who are. Once you lead them through the initial book study I mentioned before, they will self-identify for you. Those who believe what you believe will be hungry for more.

When you see a hungry team member, feed them. Give them more. To do that, you must also continuously grow.

"Everyone wants to contribute. Trust them. Leaders are everywhere. Find them. Some people are on a mission. Celebrate them. Others wish things were different. Listen to them. Everyone matters. Show them." ~ Bob Chapman

26

THE WEAK LINKS

DON'T FIRE THEM, FIRE THEM UP

"As a leader, and ultimately a mentor, you have the responsibility and privilege to grow those around you and help them become their absolute best." ~ Mike Davis

There will always be weak links on a team. As I shared in the last chapter, high impact leaders focus their energy on the top performers, not the low performers. But, the weak links are still on your team and should be given a small amount of your time and energy. So, make it count.

As the old saying goes, *"A chain is only as strong as its weakest link."* The same goes for a team. The team is only as strong as the weakest link on the team. Often, the weak link is actually the leader of the team. However, since you're reading this book, I'm going to assume you're not the weak link on your team.

Most weak links can be made strong if they are led by a high impact leader. However, managers of people do not have the necessary character to grow and develop the weak links. Most often, they won't even choose to grow and develop themselves. If they won't grow and develop themselves, how can they be expected to grow and develop others? They can't. In this case, they *are* the weak link.

As my mentor, John C. Maxwell, says, *"Insecure leaders don't develop their people. They replace them."* What a powerful and true statement. Insecure leaders, managers of people, look out the window and blame the weak links. They don't know what they don't know. They don't look in the mirror, take the blame, and admit *they* are the weak link.

Often, when I was leading teams, the formal authority, positional leader felt the need to tell me in advance who the weak links on the team were. He/she thought it would help if I knew where my greatest challenge would come from. However, I didn't let someone else's opinion of another influence the way I led them.

As I mentioned, I went in on Monday morning and believed in everyone on the team equally. I didn't assume a person who was labeled a weak link by a manager of people was really a weak link. I assumed I had a team full of stars. And guess what, with only a few exceptions across hundreds of teams, they all performed like stars. They rose to meet my expectations of them.

If I had treated the weak link like a weak link, most likely, they would have lived up to my expectation of them. I'm telling you now as a high impact leader: Don't fire them. Fire them up!

You have a weak link on your team. You may not have been able to motivate them before reading this book. But, you have a whole new toolbox now. Start from scratch with them, and apply what I've been teaching you. Focus on building a relationship and connecting with them and all the others.

You are now equipped to lead your team in an entirely new way at an entirely new level. When you get better, they will get better. You are the leader. You are responsible. Make it happen. Lead your team. All of them. As you shift your focus to the top performers, they will assist you with the weak links. As you grow and develop your team, the entire team will be better positioned to positively influence the weak links.

I've got a story about a weak link that wasn't even close to being a weak link. He was a powerhouse on my team, but he was a weak link on his leader's team. What was the difference? The weak link? No, he was the same person. He didn't change from one day to the next.

What did change? The leader. When I walked in to lead the team on Monday morning, he was put underneath my leadership umbrella for a week. My ability to lead people was far greater than his leader's ability to lead people. His leader was a manager. I am a high impact leader. Big difference.

I was warned in advance about Joe (not his real name) by his manager. I was told Joe wasn't happy we would be making changes in his area. He said Joe *really* didn't like the idea of me moving his work platform. I thought, how did Joe know I was going to move his work platform? I didn't even know that.

Understand, I had met with the manager a few weeks earlier to identify a pilot area for their first formal improvement event with me. Together, we decided on Joe's work area. The manager asked what I expected to change. I pointed out many things. One of them was the *potential* for Joe's work platform to be removed. When I left, I asked the manager to keep our thoughts confidential because the team would decide what changes to actually make, not me. I would only lead and guide them, not direct them. He agreed.

Fast forward a few weeks. I was back to lead the team. When I first walked in, Joe was angry and actually threatened me with violence. Why was he so angry with me? I had never met Joe. He proceeded to tell me what the manager had said.

To prepare him and give him time to cool off, Joe's insecure manager had told him in advance I would be removing his platform when I came back. I immediately told Joe it wouldn't be removed unless he wanted it removed. And, if it was removed without his agreement, I would never be back because I don't work with organizations that disrespect their people. I had to start building trust right away.

On Wednesday, Joe hauled it to the scrap bin himself. It was his idea. This was in 2009. He still follows me on Facebook to this day. He wasn't the weak link. His leader was.

"When you decide to pursue greatness, you are taking responsibility for your life. This means that you are choosing to accept the consequences of your actions, and to become the agent of your mental, physical, spiritual, and material success. You may not always be able to control what life puts in your path, but I believe you can always control who you are." ~ Les Brown

27

A BIGGER SACRIFICE

WILL YOU CHOOSE TO LEAD AT A HIGHER LEVEL?

"Character cannot be developed in ease and quiet. Only through experience of trial and suffering can the soul be strengthened, ambition inspired, and success achieved."
~ Helen Keller

How much are you willing to sacrifice to get from where you are to where you want to be? The answer to that question will determine how far up the leadership mountain you will climb and how many, if any, you will help climb to the top.

The moment you're done sacrificing is the moment you're done climbing. You're either moving forward or backward. There is no such thing as sitting still in the leadership world. There's always someone out there willing to pay the price when you won't. If you're no longer hungry for growth, you'll be easily passed by those who are. It's not their fault. It's *your* fault. The problem is always in the mirror.

We must give up something in order to gain something. If we want a better job, we have to sacrifice time learning and gaining experience before we get the job. Or, we must sacrifice time to get a degree before we will even be considered for the job. Moving forward doesn't just naturally occur. You must be intentional.

Once you have given up to get a job, you must now continue to give up to keep the job. What got you the job won't allow you to keep the job. You will be expected to do more and apply yourself more. Then, if you're still interested in climbing higher, you will have to repeat the cycle of sacrifice over and over again.

You may have to go back to school, work longer hours than others, invest hours at home in reading and studying in the areas of leadership development and also in your areas of competency, or what you're interested in doing.

Sacrifice is giving up something of value today for something of greater value tomorrow, next week, next month, or next year. Sacrificing today for a better future takes vision, desire, and discipline.

Without a vision of a brighter future, you will not have hope. Hope isn't a strategy, but you will need hope to develop a strategy. With hope, you can imagine how things could be. As your future begins to come into focus, you begin to have a greater desire to make it your reality.

It's that desire within you that will help you develop a plan of action. Desire will lead you to ask yourself a lot of questions. Why do I want to get there? How will I get there? Who can help me get there? When will I get there?

These are principles that apply to all of life. However, my intention is to help you grow as a leader and to help you grow and develop other leaders. Your ability to grow yourself first is the foundation required to put yourself in a position to grow and develop others.

I hope by now you have a deep understanding of *why* you need to continuously grow. If you know *why*, the next question is, *"How do you grow?"* You must become disciplined at doing the things that will make you more valuable. If you want to become more successful, don't focus on becoming more successful. Focus on becoming more valuable.

The most successful people are the most valuable people. It's also much easier to determine the things that will make you more valuable. By choosing *how* you become more valuable, you will also be choosing the type of people that will value you.

Knowing *what* you need to do or knowing *how* to do what needs to be done is not your greatest challenge. Your greatest challenge is everyone's greatest challenge. What is it? It's actually having the *discipline* to do what needs to be done.

Discipline is the bridge between knowing and doing. To become more valuable and successful, you must cross this bridge daily. The more you cross it, the more valuable you become. You knew things you needed to do to get to the next level before you read this book. Now, you know a lot more.

What's stopping you from taking action? Your willingness to make sacrifices. You must be willing to give up something else in your life. TV? Games? Partying? Wasting time? Hanging out with others who aren't going anywhere? Hunting? Fishing? Golf? Something else? What is it? You know *exactly*. There's always a tradeoff when it comes to growth.

If you want to continue to unleash your potential, you must do more than simply what is required by your employer. To intentionally grow and develop yourself into a high impact leader, you must choose to grow yourself whenever and however you can. If you don't, you'll live your life helping someone else achieve their dream, and you'll never get to live your own. High impact leaders can do both.

Most leaders do absolutely nothing to develop themselves and add value to themselves. For you and me, that's good! That makes it easy to separate ourselves and shine.

How long have you been leading others? How well are you doing at developing yourself as a leader? Do you read and study leadership regularly and consistently, or are you simply satisfied with managing? If you're not leading yourself effectively, you will never lead others effectively.

What you do at work is important, but what you do when you're not at work is more important. That's when you will truly separate yourself from the crowd, or that's where you will ensure that you will always be a part of the crowd. Will you waste time or invest time?

It's your life. It's your choice. You are free to choose your actions, but you are not free to choose the consequences that flow from those actions. What are you willing to sacrifice?

"A great leader must make the choice to put other people's needs in front of his or her own." ~ Ria Story

28

CHANGE AND TRANSFORMATION

IT'S EASIER TO CHANGE,
BUT IT'S BETTER TO TRANSFORM

"Self-mastery is the hardest job you will ever tackle. If you do not conquer self, you will be conquered by self. You may see at the same time both your best friend and your worst enemy, by simply stepping in front of the mirror."
~ Napoleon Hill

I remember conducting a leadership development session with a large group of supervisors, superintendents, and upper level managers. They were very engaged and enjoyed the class. I had been taking hundreds of their front line team members through a one week Lean Leadership Certification over the past few years.

There would usually be 20-30 people in the certification classes. In the beginning, the classes were mixed with front line team members, many leaders from all levels, and those in support roles. However, after a while, the classes were made up purely of those on the front lines because there were simply so many more of them.

We would always have a graduation on Friday with various leaders and upper management in attendance. During graduation, each participant would speak about what they got out of the program and the impact it had on them. I heard some amazing testimonies. Many began to think and act completely different during their week with me.

We would often have 30-50 people attending the graduations just to see how much people were changing and to hear what they had to say. Everyone at all levels went through this program and were amazed to see the transformations that were made in just one short week.

Let's get back to the leadership development session I was conducting with the supervisors, superintendents, and upper level managers.

At the end of the day of training, I asked them to reflect on how their team members were at the graduations. They were excited to tell me how their team members were so upbeat, so positive, and so excited to grow and develop themselves into key team players and even leaders upon graduating. They also said they didn't understand how they could change so much in one week and how they wish they would stay that way.

I asked, *"What do you mean, stay that way?"* The leaders said, *"Well, they come in here with you for a week and get fired up. But then, when they come back out in the shop, it slowly wears off, and they return back to the way they were."* I asked them to explain why they thought that happened.

They said they didn't really know. I paused for a moment. Then, I held my hands out wide to symbolically embrace those in the room and said, *"It's because of you."* Then, I let it sink in for a moment. They didn't want to take responsibility, so I helped them look in the mirror. They preferred to look out the window and find someone else to blame: their team or me.

I said, *"So, they come in with me for a week and totally change themselves. Then, go back under your leadership umbrella and slowly slip back to where they were. Is that right?"* They reluctantly said, *"Yes, that's what happens."* I already knew that was happening, and I also knew why.

I explained to the leaders the same thing had happened to them too. They had come in for a week, got fired up, and were motivated to lead their team members at a higher level. However, they simply changed that week. They did not and could not truly transform themselves during that week. As a result, they changed back to the way they were.

Their team members slipped back because of the leader's inability to lead at a high level. I unleashed their team, and they suppressed their team. They wanted the team that graduated on Friday, but they were only capable of leading the team that had entered on Monday. So, the team slowly slipped back underneath their leader's leadership umbrella after graduation.

Their leaders were not willing to pay the price of transformation. They were not willing to sacrifice in order to transform themselves into high impact leaders. Not only did they pay the bigger price of settling and coasting in their position, but so did their team members. When a leader won't pay the price, everyone on their team ends up paying the price.

When we change, we can also change back. But when we grow enough repeatedly and consistently over time, we begin to transform. Once we are truly transformed, there is no going back. What impact has *Blue-Collar Leadership*® *& Supervision* had on you? Do you want to simply make a few changes to improve your team's results? That's easy and won't require very much sacrifice. The cost is low. Or, do you want to truly transform yourself and your leadership style? That's hard and will require a lot of sacrifice. The cost will be high, but the reward will be great.

If you choose true transformation and endless growth as I did when I was exposed to my first leadership book, there will be no limit on you or the teams you will lead. Everything, personally and professionally, will change for the better and continuously get better as time passes.

However, if you choose to only change a little where it's easy and choose to pick a few principles you've learned and move on as you were, very little is going to change. Nearly everything in your life will remain the same. It's your choice.

Transformation isn't for the weak. Transformation is for the strong. Those that choose transformation will become high impact leaders and will help others choose transformation. They will impact many lives. They will truly make a difference.

What will it be for you? A change? Or, a transformation?

"When we are faced with change, we either step forward into growth, or we step backward into safety."
~ Abraham Maslow

29

TOP PERFORMERS

THE CHALLENGE OF RETAINING
YOUR GAME CHANGERS

*"Those who build great companies understand that the
ultimate throttle on growth for any great company is not
markets, or technology, or competition, or products.
It is the one thing above all others – the ability to get
and keep enough of the right people." ~ Jim Collins*

Why do most people leave the team, department, or the
organization? There are many reasons people leave, but the
primary reason is related to the relationship with their boss.
People tend to stay or leave because of how their boss makes
them feel. Do they feel like they matter? Do they feel valued?

I'm sure you can validate this for yourself. When you've left
a job, a department, or a company, was the most common
reason because of the relationship between you and your boss?
Or, when your friends and family have left jobs, did you hear a
lot of discussion around their relationship with their boss?

There's something actually worse and more common than
having a team member leave. That's having them quit
emotionally but stay physically. When they *quit but stay*, it's the
leader's responsibility to remove them from the team as quickly
as possible because they will only contaminate the team and
cause problems. While they're on the team, your leadership will
be questioned, and you will lose trust with the other team
members, especially the top performers. To retain the best,
remove the worst.

When you keep low performing, problem causing team
members on the team you risk losing your top performers.

Since they are top performers, they usually have options. Other departments will want them, and other companies will want them. The question you must ask yourself is, *"How bad do I want to keep them?"*

I've seen a lot of high performers leave a team when they didn't really want to leave. I've also been one of them. I've had others who decided to leave talk to me about it in advance. I've seen them struggle with staying or leaving. But, they become very miserable and unhappy working alongside people who decided to quit but stay. They are most upset by their leader's willingness to allow the low performers to contaminate the team.

Managers of people will not make the tough decisions that will best serve the team. Instead of removing the slackers, they allow them to stay which hurts the performance of the entire team. The reason managers don't remove them is because of the burden it will cause them personally. They will have to go through the hiring and training process and often must fill in on the job until they find a replacement. Most managers choose the easy way out and keep the low performer.

However, a high impact leader realizes the damage being done. They will act quickly. They can't get the slacker out of the way fast enough. They don't mind filling in if necessary and embrace the opportunity to find a new team member with a better fit for the team. As a result, the team's morale is lifted and respect for their leader increases. The team rewards the leader's decision by working hard to help cover for the missing team member because they appreciate the leader's willingness to do the right thing. When this happens, the top performers are usually leading the charge.

One of the best ways to retain top performers is to work very intentionally to build a high performance team. I've already shared many of the principles you'll need to apply in order to do so. When people are attracted to the leader *and* the team, there is a greater chance of retaining them. Creating a team that works well together, values each other, supports the leader, and the organization isn't an easy task, but it's necessary to attract and retain top performers.

A low performing leader can't build a high performance team. The lower your level of leadership, the lower your team's performance. In order to attract and retain top performers, you must be a top performer yourself. In other words, you must be a high impact leader.

As you become a better leader, you will begin to attract and retain better followers and increase your odds of keeping those you do attract. However, as a high impact leader, you will find yourself happy to grow and develop leaders that will either take your position as you move on or fill other positions as they become available in other areas. And when they do, you'll be proud you played a small role in helping them get to the next level. Hopefully, you can keep them in the company.

I remember a young supervisor in a welding department who really bought into my onsite leadership development classes. He was a star from the beginning. He wanted to move up in the company. He followed my advice and worked to build his team. He approached it in two ways.

First, he focused on helping everyone improve. Second, he intentionally helped those who wanted to move up in the company do so. He was their biggest cheerleader. He became known for growing and developing leaders. He would grow and develop his team members, then help them fill jobs in other areas. Those who stayed with him wanted to stay with him and loved what they were doing.

When a leadership position above him opened up, he was selected. He also already had his replacement trained and ready to fill his spot instantly. Many of the leaders he had helped grow and develop, now reported to him once again in his new role. You can imagine the support and loyalty he had from those he had helped move forward. They already knew his heart and wanted to help him succeed.

When a high impact leader is leading a team, everyone wins.

"It is the future that pulls rather than the past that pushes."
~ Peter Koestenbaum

30

THE ULTIMATE QUESTION

WILL YOU BE AN INFORMER
OR A TRANSFORMER?

*"I am not what happened to me,
I am what I choose to become." ~ Carl Jung*

It is my hope that you have learned a lot, thought a lot, and reflected a lot as you have read this book. You have so much more potential. How do I know? Because we all do. It's why I wrote this book. I know I can make a bigger difference, and I feel responsible for doing so. I hope you will step up and help me grow and develop more high impact leaders.

I hope I have inspired you to realize your team, your organization, your community, your country, and our world need you to continue to climb the leadership mountain. Our world is desperate for leaders that will step up, lead at a higher level, and make a bigger difference from wherever they are. I believe you are one of those leaders. You're still reading because there's something in you that is aligned with the principles I've been sharing. That something in you is a leader.

Will you inform others or transform others? Will you simply pass along information? Or, will you passionately pass along inspiration. Managers are informers, but high impact leaders are transformers.

Managers change processes and procedures, not themselves. They are focused on the job and the results, not the people. They are goal oriented.

High impact leaders inspire people to make positive changes in their lives. They are focused on the people. They model what they expect from others. They are growth oriented, not goal oriented. High impact leaders live with purpose on purpose for a purpose.

You *can* be a transformer. But, *will* you be a transformer? That's a question only you can answer. It reminds me of something I read in my friend, Amir Ghannad's book, *The Transformative Leader*. Amir had this to say, *"Your transformation will not come from what I tell you, but from what you tell yourself and ultimately what you do."*

All I can do is influence you and encourage you to do the same for others as you learn and grow. I hope I've inspired you to lead your group through a 30 day book study using *Blue-Collar Leadership®: Leading from the Front Lines*. If so, you are well on your way to transforming yourself as a leader and helping your team members become high impact followers. Once they've mastered followership, they will be prepared to climb higher on their own personal leadership journey.

I encourage you to live with abundance as you choose to become a transformer of people. Not only can you grow and develop your team, you can also grow and develop your peers. Are you willing to step up and lead your peers? Remember, leadership is influence. You don't need authority.

If you've enjoyed this book, volunteer to lead your peers through a book study on this content and encourage them to lead their teams through book studies as well. Most companies are happy to supply resources to those on their team who want to grow and develop themselves and others. Usually, all you have to do is ask. Then, let them see you shine.

If you overcome your fears and truly become intentional, you will get noticed and will quickly become known as a high impact leader within your organization. Do this often enough, and long enough, and you will be amazed at the opportunities you will be given to lead and to make a bigger impact within the organization.

The degree in which you're able to transform yourself will determine your ability to transform others. You must first learn it. Then, you must apply it, live it, and teach it to others. Don't expect your world to change overnight. However, you should expect it to change drastically over months and years.

If this was your first leadership book, I want you to know I'm proud of you and hope it has impacted you as much as my first one impacted me. My goal from the beginning was to write something on these pages that would inspire you to make a change for the better.

I also intended to help you jumpstart your growth by revealing things to you I didn't learn until 20 or 30 years into my career. If you truly want to learn what I've shared with you on these pages, start teaching it to others. Share a quote. Take the book to work with you and share some highlights. Inspire your organization to start a formal leadership development program.

If they're not interested, that's okay. But, don't let that stop you from making it happen wherever you are. All you must do is apply what you're learning and start getting amazing results. When you do, others will want to know what's going on. When they ask, they will be opening the door for you to begin leveraging your influence with your answer.

Patience is the key when introducing formal leadership into an organization. There are many high level leaders that have never read a leadership book. You're now ahead of all of those. Let your example provide the proof of how powerful and transformational these principles can be. Make it happen!

"Death is not the greatest loss in life. The greatest loss is what dies inside us while we live." ~ Norman Cousins

I welcome hearing how this book has influenced the way you think, the way you lead, or the results you have achieved because of what you've learned in it. Please feel free to share your thoughts with me by email at:

Mack@MackStory.com

To order my books, audio books, and other resources, please visit: BlueCollarLeadership.com or Amazon.com

ABOUT THE AUTHOR

Mack's story is an amazing journey of personal and professional growth. He married Ria in 2001. He has one son, Eric, born in 1991.

After graduating high school in 1987, Mack joined the United States Marine Corps Reserve as an 0311 infantryman. Soon after, he began his 20 plus year manufacturing career. Graduating with highest honors, he earned an Executive Bachelor of Business Administration degree from Faulkner University.

Mack began his career in manufacturing in 1988 on the front lines of a large production machine shop. He eventually grew himself into upper management and found his niche in lean manufacturing and along with it, developed his passion for leadership. In 2008, he launched his own Lean Manufacturing and Leadership Development firm.

From 2005-2012, Mack led leaders and their cross-functional teams through more than 11,000 hours of process improvement, organizational change, and cultural transformation. Ria joined Mack full-time in late 2013.

In 2013, they worked with John C. Maxwell as part of an international training event focused on the Cultural Transformation in Guatemala where over 20,000 leaders were trained. They also shared the stage with internationally recognized motivational speaker Les Brown in 2014.

Mack and Ria have published 20+ books on personal growth and leadership development and publish more each year. In 2018, they reached 66,000 international followers on LinkedIn where they provide daily motivational, inspirational, and leadership content to people all over the world.

Clients: ATD (Association for Talent Development), Auburn University, Chevron, Chick-fil-A, Kimberly Clark, Koch Industries, Southern Company, and the U.S. Military.

Mack is an inspiration for people everywhere as an example of achievement, growth, and personal development. His passion motivates and inspires people all over the world!

WHAT WE OFFER:

- ✓ Keynote Speaking: Conferences, Seminars, Onsite
- ✓ Workshops: Onsite/Offsite Half/Full/Multi Day
- ✓ Leadership Development Support: Leadership, Teamwork, Personal Growth, Organizational Change, Planning, Executing, Trust, Cultural Transformation, Communication, Time Management, Selling with Character, Resilience, & Relationship Building
- ✓ Blue-Collar Leadership® Development
- ✓ Corporate Retreats
- ✓ Women's Retreat (with Ria Story)
- ✓ Limited one-on-one coaching/mentoring
- ✓ On-site Lean Leadership Certification
- ✓ Lean Leader Leadership Development
- ✓ Become licensed to teach our content

FOR MORE INFORMATION PLEASE VISIT:

BlueCollarLeadership.com
TopStoryLeadership.com

FOLLOW US ON SOCIAL MEDIA:

LinkedIn.com/in/MackStory
Facebook.com/Mack.Story

LinkedIn.com/in/RiaStory
Facebook.com/Ria.Story

LISTEN/SUBSCRIBE TO OUR PODCASTS AT:

Mack Story: Anchor.fm/BlueCollarLeadership
Ria Story: Anchor.fm/RiaStory

Excerpt (Trait 3 of 30) from
Blue-Collar Leadership® & Teamwork:
30 Traits of High Impact Players

BE RESPONSIBLE

MAKING THIS CHOICE GIVES YOU A VOICE

"Total responsibility for failure is a difficult thing to accept, and taking ownership when things go wrong requires extraordinary humility and courage."
~ Jocko Willink

The higher we climb up the organizational chart or the higher we climb up the pay scale, the harder it is for many of us to remain humble. However, as high impact team players, it's our responsibility to choose to be humble regardless of our status or income. And if necessary, it's also our responsibility to learn what it truly means to be humble.

Humility is a choice that high impact players will make.

If you haven't accomplished much or done much, it's a little easier to remain humble. I believe as a whole the blue-collar workforce is naturally more humble simply because of who we are and where we come from. However, I also believe some who climb their way up from the entry-level positions let it go to their heads.

I want to remain a humble high impact player. That's on me. Not letting my success go to my head is my responsibility. I've also gone a step farther and made helping others do the same my responsibility. High impact team players always do more than is required.

Each of us is responsible for choosing our values and

those values will determine our circumstances and the impact we have, especially when it comes to teamwork.

Just as humility is sometimes a hard choice for those with a high position or status, taking responsibility is often a hard choice for those in a low position or status. But as I've learned over the years, taking responsibility seems to be a hard choice for many regardless of their title, position, rank, status, or income.

When it comes to teamwork, low impact players dodge responsibility like it's a deadly disease. They may disappear when the task is being addressed or begin to make excuses as to why they can't help and shouldn't be asked to help. That creates distrust.

High impact players know a secret: When low impact players are whining, it's easy to start shining. They also know how to shine. It's actually pretty simple. They just listen for whining, and then step up and say, "I'll do it."

At that moment, the high impact player builds trust by simply taking the responsibility. The next responsibility of the high impact player is to follow through and get results. If they don't, they will create distrust with the team and the leaders. If they do, they will build additional trust with the team and the leaders.

Leaders are ultimately responsible for making things happen. If they don't make things happen, it won't be long before they are replaced by someone else who will be given the same mission. High impact players know the quickest way to build trust with a leader is to help them get results, so that's what they focus on doing.

As they develop a reputation for helping the leaders get results, their influence increases with those leaders. Because of their choice (taking responsibility and following through), they earn a voice. As time passes, the high impact players are asked their opinions much more often than the low impact players.

As a result, the high impact players begin to influence the leader's choices and the team's direction. They're still on the team, but they're playing at much higher level. Those who are willing to make things happen are also given more chances to make things happen.

High impact players are never just along for the ride. They want to drive. They see the big picture. They don't shy away from responsibility. They wake up everyday looking for an opportunity to shine.

Imagine a team full of low impact players where everyone is dodging responsibility on every front. The leader will be frustrated, and the team will be frustrated. And little, if anything, will get accomplished. Unfortunately, these types of teams are common. Depending on your circumstances, it may be too easy to imagine this team. If so, don't miss what's right in front of you: endless opportunities to shine.

Now imagine a very different team, one filled with high impact players. They could be given the exact same mission as the frustrated low impact team. However, no one would be frustrated. The mission would be accomplished. Instead of being focused on finding excuses, the entire team would be focused on finding a way to make it happen. In that case, everyone shines.

What's the major difference between the two teams above? Attitude. Low impact players tend to have a negative attitude. High impact players always have a positive attitude. Attitude is a choice. If we can choose to be positive or negative, why not choose to be positive.

"Responsibility includes two important ideas –
choosing right over wrong and accepting ownership
for one's conduct and obligations." ~ Charles G. Koch

Excerpt (Ch. 5 of 30) from
Blue-Collar Leadership®:
Leading from the Front Lines

THERE IS AN "I" IN TEAM

EVERY TEAM IS MADE OF "I"NDIVIDUALS

"I'm just a plowhand from Arkansas, but I have learned how to hold a team together – how to lift some men up, how to calm others down, until finally they've got one heartbeat together as a team. There's always just three things I say: 'If anything goes bad, I did it. If anything goes semi-good, then we did it. If anything goes real good, they did it.' That's all it takes to get people to win." ~ Paul "Bear" Bryant

Paul *"Bear"* Bryant was one of the greatest college football coaches to ever lead a team of young men down the field. He was also a *"plowhand"* from Arkansas. A blue-collar worker. The blue-collar world has produced some of the greatest leaders of all time, so you should be proud and hold your head high. *Without them, the world as we know it would not exist.*

There's nothing holding you back but you. As my blue-collar friend, Donovan Weldon, stated so well, *"The only person between you and success is you. MOVE! The only person between you and failure is you. STAND FIRM!"* Those are strong words of wisdom. Donovan started on the bottom just like you and me. But today, he's the CEO of Donovan Industrial Service in Orange, TX near Beaumont.

Donovan's success didn't happen by accident. He made it happen. You can make things happen too! He's a blue-collar leader that believes in and develops his team on a regular basis. I know because my wife, Ria, and I had the privilege of being brought in to speak to his team about leadership in 2014. They are making it happen on purpose for a purpose!

It's time for you to stop playing small and start playing tall.

A college degree is not required for you to play at a higher level. Not having one is simply an excuse some people use to continue playing small. If you want a college degree, use what you will learn on these pages to find a way to get one. If you don't want a college degree, use what you learn on these pages to make it happen without one.

You are the key to your success. You must believe in yourself. You must grow and develop yourself, which is what you're doing as you read this book. Do not stop growing! And when the time is right, you must bet on yourself.

Understanding your role as a team member is another must. Those on the front lines often underestimate themselves because they can't see the big picture. They can't see the value they have to offer. Far too often, their boss isn't a high impact leader and needs a lot of growth and development too. Bosses are often given the title without any formal development.

When I write about the front lines on these pages, I'm not only talking about the people in entry level positions. They are obviously on the front lines, but they also have leaders that are on the front lines with them and various team members supporting them too. They can all learn from these pages.

This book was written specifically for anyone at any level that visits, interacts with, or works on the front lines.

The principles I share with you must be applied if you want to make a high impact and be recognized for leading from the front lines. Regardless of your position, the more you apply these principles, the more options you will have, and the more positions you will be offered as you climb even higher.

Teams are made up of "I"ndividuals, so there are many I's on every team, regardless of how many times you hear, *"There is no 'I' in TEAM."* As a matter of fact, *you are one of them.* Every person on a team is an "I" and has the potential to lead (influence) the team, positively or negatively.

"Leadership is influence. Nothing more. Nothing less."
~ John C. Maxwell

You must understand there are many official and unofficial teams in the organization where you work. They are very dynamic and constantly changing.

When most of us think of which team we are on, we immediately think of our peers, the ones on the same crew, in the same department, or working on the same job. This is our core team, but it only represents the smallest team we're on. We also support other teams too, as others support our team.

When we choose to contribute beyond our immediate team, we are choosing to be part of a bigger team. Often, this only requires a choice to do so. Your choice to get involved in other areas sends a clear message to the high impact leaders.

When you play tall, you choose to contribute because you know it will increase your influence and your impact on the front lines. If you want to play tall, you should want to be noticed, to be selected, to volunteer, to share information, to accept more responsibility, and ultimately, to make a contribution at a higher level.

As a direct result of your choice to step up, your influence increases. You're demonstrating you can lead from the front lines and will be seen and respected by all high impact leaders as a high impact leader. Your actions will not go unnoticed.

When you play small, you choose not to contribute because you don't want to do more. If your goal is to coast until pay day, it won't be a secret you can keep. When you make every effort not to be noticed, not to be selected, not to volunteer, not to share information, not to accept responsibility, and ultimately to not contribute, *you will absolutely be noticed*.

As a direct result of your choice not to step up, your influence decreases. Your influence on the front lines and with your leaders will be diminished. You are more likely to become reactive and frustrated blaming others for what you have chosen. Blaming others will further reduce your influence.

You first make your choices, then your choices make you.

"The most valuable player is the one that makes the most players valuable." ~ Peyton Manning

Excerpt (Ch. 26 of 30) from
***Blue-Collar Kaizen:
Leading Lean & Lean Teams***

LEVERAGE THE TEAM

FOCUS ON STRENGTHS;
DEVELOP WEAKNESSES

*"Instead of focusing on weaknesses, give your
attention to people's strengths. Focus on sharpening
skills that already exist. Compliment positive qualities.
Bring out the gifts inherent in them. Weaknesses can
wait unless they are character flaws. Only after you
have developed a strong rapport with the person and
they have begun to grow and gain confidence should
you address areas of weakness...and then those
should be handled gently and one at a time."*
~ John C. Maxwell

High impact Lean leaders have a gift for turning a
group of people into a team in a short period of time.

At the start of a kaizen event, calling the group of
people a team is a poor use of the word team. They are
simply a group of people assembled in a room about to
be given a task to accomplish together. Most often, some
want to be there, and some don't want to be there. Odds
are, this specific group of people has never worked
together on a project before.

Knowing about continuous improvement is a must if
you're going to lead a kaizen event. However, knowing
about continuous improvement (your competency) will
not be the key to turning a group of people into a team of
people. Turning a group of people into a team of people

is about having respect for the people. Your ability to quickly build a strong, functional team will be determined primarily by your character and secondarily by your competency. Your character is key in this area.

I've seen some very talented Lean leaders and others who have an extensive in-depth knowledge of Lean attempt to lead kaizen events. Most often, they struggle from the moment the event kicks off until the end. They know a lot about Lean but very little about leading people effectively. Why? Because their focus has been on learning Lean, not on learning leadership.

When it comes to growing, developing, and creating a new team, high impact Lean leaders know to focus on the team member's strengths in their area of competency and to develop their weaknesses in the area of character.

Each team member's competency strengths (what they know and can do), if leveraged, will launch the team forward. Each team member's character weaknesses (who they are) will hold the team back. This includes you.

High impact Lean leaders know there are always character issues. We all have them. A few of us are constantly working to improving ourselves, but many of us aren't. Focusing on character weaknesses is why high impact Lean leaders blend leadership development and personal growth components into all of their continuous improvement initiatives.

This is why I utilize the 20/80 rule I taught you in chapter 19. I didn't start using it by accident. I started using it by design. Until then, I only focused on leveraging the team's strengths. But, I hadn't been focused on developing their weaknesses. I'm sure you already know the root cause of most major problems that arise during kaizen events, whether with team members or people not on the team, is rooted in character issues.

The majority of Lean leaders focus only on the continuous improvement (competency) component of Lean. As a result, they provide no leadership in the area that will hold them and the team back the most, character development.

The reason Lean leaders do not address character development during kaizen events is because many of them are not addressing it in their own lives. In other words, because they are not leading themselves well, they cannot lead others well. Character development is always the missing link personally and professionally.

In the area of competency, ask questions and generate discussions to find out what people like or don't like to do. Don't assume they like to do what they are paid to do. I always have everyone introduce and speak about themselves before I talk about anything. I ask what their job is, how long they have been with the organization, what their previous job was, what their hobbies are, what they do for fun, how much Lean and event experience they have, and I ask them to tell me about their family.

The answers to these questions and the associated discussions allow me to connect and learn about their strengths. Then, I'm positioned to leverage the team.

"Humility means knowing and using your strength for the benefit of others, on behalf of a higher purpose. The humble leader is not weak, but strong...is not pre-occupied with self, but with how best to use his or her strengths for the good of others. A humble leader does not think less of himself, but chooses to consider the needs of others in fulfilling a worthy cause. We love to be in the presence of a humble leader because they bring out the very best in us. Their focus is on our purpose, our contribution, and our ability to accomplish all we set out to accomplish." ~ Alan Ross

Order books online at Amazon or BlueCollarLeadership.com

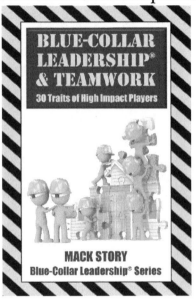

Are you ready to play at the next level and beyond?

In today's high stakes game of business, the players on the team are the competitive advantage for any organization. But, only if they are on the field instead of on the bench.

The competitive advantage for every individual is developing 360° of influence regardless of position, title, or rank.

Blue-Collar Leadership® & Teamwork provides a simple, yet powerful and unique, resource for individuals who want to increase their influence and make a high impact. It's also a resource and tool for leaders, teams, and organizations, who are ready to Engage the Front Line to Improve the Bottom Line.

Order books online at Amazon or BlueCollarLeadership.com

"I wish someone had given me these books 30 years ago when I started my career on the front lines. They would have changed my life then. They can change your life now." ~ Mack Story

Blue-Collar Leadership® *& Supervision* and *Blue-Collar Leadership*® are written specifically for those who lead the people on the frontlines and for those on the front lines. With 30 short, easy to read 3 page chapters, these books contain powerful, yet simple to understand leadership lessons.

Note: These two Blue-Collar Leadership® *books are the blue-collar version of the MAXIMIZE books and contain nearly identical content.*

**Down load the first 5 chapters of each book FREE at:
BlueCollarLeadership.com**

Order books online at Amazon or BlueCollarLeadership.com

The biggest challenge in process improvement and cultural transformation isn't identifying the problems. It's execution: implementing and sustaining the solutions.

Blue-Collar Kaizen is a resource for anyone in any position who is, or will be, leading a team through process improvement and change. Learn to engage, empower, and encourage your team for long term buy-in and sustained gains.

Mack Story has over 11,000 hours experience leading hundreds of leaders and thousands of their cross-functional kaizen team members through process improvement, organizational change, and cultural transformation. He shares lessons learned from his experience and many years of studying, teaching, and applying leadership principles.

Order books online at Amazon or TopStoryLeadership.com

High impact leaders align their habits with key values in order to maximize their influence. High impact leaders intentionally grow and develop themselves in an effort to more effectively grow and develop others.

These *10 Values* are commonly understood. However, they are not always commonly practiced. These *10 Values* will help you build trust and accelerate relationship building. Those mastering these *10 Values* will be able to lead with speed as they develop 360° of influence from wherever they are.

Order books online at Amazon or TopStoryLeadership.com

Are you looking for transformation in your life? Do you want better results? Do you want stronger relationships?

In *Defining Influence*, Mack breaks down many of the principles that will allow anyone at any level to methodically and intentionally increase their positive influence.

Mack blends his personal growth journey with lessons on the principles he learned along the way. He's not telling you what he learned after years of research, but rather what he learned from years of application and transformation. Everything rises and falls on influence.

Order books online at Amazon or TopStoryLeadership.com

10 Foundational Elements of Intentional Transformation serves as a source of motivation and inspiration to help you climb your way to the next level and beyond as you learn to intentionally create a better future for yourself. The pages will ENCOURAGE, ENGAGE, and EMPOWER you as you become more focused and intentional about moving from where you are to where you want to be.

All of us are somewhere, but most of us want to be somewhere else. However, we don't always know how to get there. You will learn how to intentionally move forward as you learn to navigate the 10 foundational layers of transformation.

Order books online at Amazon or TopStoryLeadership.com

"Sales persuasion and influence, moving others, has changed more in the last 10 years than it has in the last 100 years. It has transitioned from buyer beware to seller beware" ~ *Daniel Pink*

So, it's no longer *"Buyer beware!"* It's *"Seller beware!"* Why? Today, the buyer has the advantage over the seller. Most often, they are holding it in their hand. It's a smart phone. They can learn everything about your product before they meet you. They can compare features and prices instantly. The major advantage you do still have is: YOU! IF they like you. IF they trust you. IF they feel you want to help them.

This book is filled with 30 short chapters providing unique insights that will give you the advantage, not over the buyer, but over your competition: those who are selling what you're selling. It will help you sell yourself.

Order books online at Amazon or TopStoryLeadership.com

"I wish someone had given me these books 30 years ago when I started my career. They would have changed my life then. They can change your life now." ~ *Mack Story*

MAXIMIZE Your Potential will help you learn to lead yourself well. *MAXIMIZE Your Leadership Potential* will help you learn to lead others well. With 30 short, easy to read 3 page chapters, these books contain simple and easy to understand, yet powerful leadership lessons.

Note: These two MAXIMIZE books are the white-collar, or non-specific, version of the Blue-Collar Leadership® books and contain nearly identical content.

ABOUT RIA STORY

Mack's wife, Ria, is also a motivational leadership speaker, author, and a world class coach who has a unique ability to help people develop and achieve their life and career goals, and guide them in building the habits and discipline to achieve their personal view of greatness. Ria brings a wealth of personal experience in working with clients to achieve their personal goals and aspirations in a way few coaches can.

Like many, Ria has faced adversity in life. Raised on an isolated farm in Alabama, she suffered extreme sexual abuse by her father from age 12 to 19. Desperate to escape, she left home at 19 without a job, a car, or even a high school diploma. Ria learned to be resilient, and not just survive, but thrive. (Watch her 7 minute TEDx talk at RiaStory.com/TEDx) She worked her way through school, acquiring an MBA with a 4.0 GPA, and eventually resigned from her career in the corporate world to pursue a passion for helping others achieve success.

Ria's background includes more than 10 years in healthcare administration, including several years in management, and later, Director of Compliance and Regulatory Affairs for a large healthcare organization. Ria's responsibilities included oversight of thousands of organizational policies, organizational compliance with all State and Federal regulations, and responsibility for several million dollars in Medicare appeals.

Ria co-founded Top Story Leadership, which offers leadership speaking, training, coaching, and consulting.

Ria's Story From Ashes To Beauty
by Ria Story

The unforgettable story and inspirational memoir of a young woman who was extremely sexually abused by her father from age 12 to 19 and then rejected by her mother. (Watch 7 minutes of her story in her TEDx talk at RiaStory.com/TEDx)

For the first time, Ria publicly reveals details of the extreme sexual abuse she endured growing up. 13 years after leaving home at 19, she decided to speak out about her story and encourage others to find hope and healing.

Determined to not only survive, but also thrive, Ria shares how she was able to overcome the odds and find hope and healing to Achieve Abundant Life. She shares the leadership principles she applied to find professional success, personal significance, and details how she was able to find the courage to share her story to give hope to others around the world.

Ria states, *"It would be easier for me to let this story go untold forever and simply move on with life…One of the most difficult things I've ever done is write this book. Victims of sexual assault or abuse don't want to talk because they want to avoid the social stigma and the fear of not being believed or the possibility of being blamed for something that was not their fault. My hope and prayer is someone will benefit from learning how I was able to overcome such difficult circumstances. That brings purpose to the pain and reason enough to share what I would rather have left behind forever. Our scars make us stronger."*

Available at Amazon.com in paperback, audio, and eBook. To order your signed copy, to learn more about Ria, or to book her to speak at your event, please visit: RiaStory.com/TEDx

Order books online at Amazon or RiaStory.com

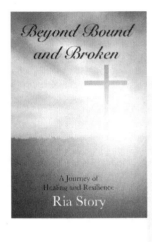

Ria Story

In *Beyond Bound and Broken*, Ria shares how she overcame the shame, fear, and doubt she developed after enduring years of extreme sexual abuse by her father. Forced to play the role of a wife and even shared with other men due to her father's perversions, Ria left home at 19 without a job, a car, or even a high-school diploma. This book also contains lessons on resilience and overcoming adversity that you can apply to your own life.

In *Ria's Story From Ashes To Beauty*, Ria tells her personal story of growing up as a victim of extreme sexual abuse from age 12 – 19, leaving home to escape, and her decision to tell her story. She shares her heart in an attempt to help others overcome their own adversity.

Order books online at Amazon or RiaStory.com

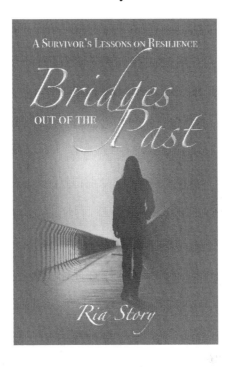

It's not what happens to you in life. It's who you become because of it. We all experience pain, grief, and loss in life. Resilience is the difference between *"I didn't die,"* and *"I learned to live again."* In this captivating book on resilience, Ria walks you through her own horrific story of more than seven years of sexual abuse by her father. She then shares how she learned not only to survive, but also to thrive in spite of her past. Learn how to overcome challenges, obstacles, and adversity in your own life by building a bridge out of the past and into the future.

(Watch 7 minutes of her story at RiaStory.com/TEDx)

Order books online at Amazon or RiaStory.com

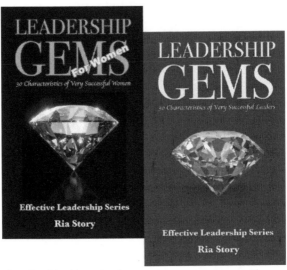

Note: Leadership Gems is the generic, non-gender specific, version of Leadership Gems for Women. The content is very similar.

Women are naturally high level leaders because they are relationship oriented. However, it's a *"man's world"* out there and natural ability isn't enough to help you be successful as a leader. You must be intentional.

Ria packed these books with 30 leadership gems which very successful people internalize and apply. Ria has combined her years of experience in leadership roles of different organizations along with years of studying, teaching, training, and speaking on leadership to give you these 30, short and simple, yet powerful and profound, lessons to help you become very successful, regardless of whether you are in a formal leadership position or not.

Order books online at Amazon or RiaStory.com

Become inspired by this 30-day collection of daily devotions for women, where you will find practical advice on intentionally living with a grateful heart, inspirational quotes, short journaling opportunities, and scripture from God's Word on practicing gratitude.

Order books online at Amazon or RiaStory.com

Ria's *Effective Leadership Series* books are written to develop and enhance your leadership skills, while also helping you increase your abilities in areas like communication and relationships, time management, planning and execution, leading and implementing change. Look for more books in the *Effective Leadership Series*:

- *Straight Talk: The Power of Effective Communication*

- *PRIME Time: The Power of Effective Planning*

- *Change Happens: Leading Yourself and Others through Change (Co-authored by Ria & Mack Story)*

Top Story Leadership
Powerful Leadership - Simplified

➢ Certified Speakers and Trainers
➢ Published Authors – 20 books available on leadership and inspirational topics
➢ Custom Leadership Programs

Keynote Speaking and Training:

Leadership Development/Personal Growth
Organizational Change/Transformation
Communication/Trust/Relationships
Time Management/Planning/Execution

Engage, Educate, and Empower
Your Audience or Team!

"Mack and Ria understand people! The dynamic team made such an impact on our front line supervision that they were begging for more training! We highly recommend Mack and Ria!" Rebecca, Director Process Improvement, GKN

"We would highly recommend Mack and Ria as speakers...their presentation was inspirational, thought-provoking, and filled with humor. They taught us some foundational leadership principles." Stephen, President-elect, WCR

TopStoryLeadership.com
Email: info@TopStoryLeadership.com

117

ENGAGE Your
FRONT LINE
To IMPROVE the
BOTTOM LINE!

If you're willing to invest in your
Blue-Collar team, I am too!

~Mack Story

Limited Time Special Offer:

Purchase books* from our Blue-Collar
Leadership® Series and receive up to 4
hours COMPLIMENTARY, on site, leadership
development training! For details, visit:

BlueCollarLeadership.com/Special-Offer

*Restrictions apply.

*"My first words are, GET SIGNED UP! This
training is not, and I stress, not your everyday
leadership seminar!" Sam, VP & COO*

118

23572844R00070

Made in the USA
Columbia, SC
13 August 2018